UNIVERSITY OF GEORGIA MONOGRAPHS, NO. 7

William Gilmore Simms
As Literary Critic

by

EDD WINFIELD PARKS

DEPAR~~~~~T OF ENGLISH
UNI~~~~~

UNIVERSITY OF GEORGIA PRESS
ATHENS   1961

UNIVERSITY OF GEORGIA MONOGRAPHS, NO. 7

William Gilmore Simms
As Literary Critic

by

EDD WINFIELD PARKS

DEPARTMENT OF ENGLISH
UNIVERSITY OF GEORGIA

UNIVERSITY OF GEORGIA PRESS
ATHENS   1961

To

GEORGE HUGH BOYD

and

JOHN OLIN EIDSON

Good friends, scholars, and colleagues

Copyright © 1961
by University of Georgia Press
Library of Congress Catalog Card Number: 61-9795
Printed in the United States of America

Contents

Preface

THIS monograph was originally intended to be a chapter in a book on ante-bellum Southern critics. But Simms wrote so much criticism which was interesting and excellent that it seemed wiser to attempt to survey this part of his work as completely as possible, rather than to compress the abundance of material into a workable chapter. Whenever possible, I have quoted directly from Simms, and have tried scrupulously to follow his punctuation and capitalization, his frequent use of italics for emphasis, and his spelling. For the sake of uniformity I have tried to conform in my own writing to his usage: since he spelled the name consistently Shakspeare, I have accepted his spelling, although at least twice, in quotations from other writers, I have used their spelling. I have attempted to avoid the necessary but somewhat loathsome *sic*, although on occasion it has been needed; but in such standard Nineteenth-Century spelling as *etherial*, and in punctuation, I have disregarded it.

I first became interested in Southern Literary Criticism in 1935, when Harry Hayden Clark suggested that in an anthology, *Southern Poets*, I should treat the critical theories of Southern poets, and include an appendix quoting the theories of various Southern poets. In no sense is Dr. Clark responsible for this monograph, but I am grateful to him for the encouragement that he has given to me. Perhaps I should mention that he has recently directed a dissertation on Simms as editor and critic by Edward T. Herbert; I have read it since my own work was practically finished, and found it sound enough, but I do not believe that it conflicts with what I have done.

This volume on Simms as critic is meant to be the first volume of a more elaborate study on ante-bellum Southern Critics. The typescript of the second volume (exclusive of Poe) has already been given to the publisher. I hope soon to complete the monograph on Poe as Critic, and thus complete this work.

In the preparation of the monograph on Simms as Critic, and even more on the entire project, I am indebted to many people. It is a pleasure to list, first of all, Mary C. Simms Oliphant. She has made freely available to me both her extensive private collection of Simms material and the manuscripts deposited in the South Caroliniana Library of the University of South Carolina. She and her sisters, Mrs. Cole and Mrs. Buck, entertained my wife and me in their home at Greenville, and also at Woodlands. Mrs. Oliphant read the manuscript and made several valuable suggestions, but never once did she suggest that anything derogatory to Simms be omitted.

Two of my colleagues, John Olin Eidson and Rayburn Moore, and Hugh Holman of the University of North Carolina, likewise read the manuscript; Edwin M. Everett read several sections of it. Each made useful and usable suggestions which I have incorporated in the work. I am grateful to them for their aid. It is also pleasant to pay tribute to Jay B. Hubbell and to his invaluable work in the field of Southern Literature. I am also indebted to Mr. A. S. Salley for making available to me his private collection of Simms' work—it too is now in the South Caroliniana Library.

Without the generous assistance of several libraries and librarians this work would have been vastly more difficult. Porter Kellam, John Bonner, John Marshall and other staff-members of the University of Georgia Library have given me constant and intelligent help throughout the work; E. L. Inabinett, Director of the South Caroliniana Library, and Ben Powell and Jay B. Hubbell, Jr., of the Duke University Library, have courteously and efficiently helped me in the use of their extensive manuscript collections. For the opportunity of working in these and other libraries, I am indebted to the M. G. Michael Award of the University of Georgia; this assistance has helped to make possible the completion of this monograph.

Two parts of this study have been previously published: the first chapter, in essentially the same form, in the *Georgia Review;* the section on Simms' editing of the Shakspeare Apocrypha is condensed from a longer article that appeared in *Studies in Shakespeare* (University of Miami Press, 1953).

Most of all, for unflagging help with the research, for intelligent criticism of the writing, and for steadying encouragement, I am grateful to my wife, Aileen Wells Parks.

E. W. P.

CHAPTER I

Simms Self-Revealed

FEW men have ever revealed themselves more completely in their letters[1] than William Gilmore Simms did. Mainly this is traceable to his own temperament: as he noted, he was without reserve in the company of people he liked and trusted, or in the letters he wrote to them. Most of his letters were written without guile or premeditation, and are therefore in essence trustworthy. They are not literary masterpieces. Partly this can be traced to his habit of hasty writing: Simms rarely if ever planned and frequently did not read over his letters, with the result that each expresses freely what Simms was thinking at the moment. He did not go back over them to qualify, strengthen, soften, or distort his opinions; instead he wrote, in one of his favorite phrases, *stans pede in uno*. As a result, he uses repeatedly certain pet phrases, quotations, and misquotations: when despondent about his writing he seems to himself to be "drawing water in a sieve"; when completing some task he is "closing rivets up"; when his or a friend's wife is pregnant, she is "As women wish to be who love their lords." These are but minor blemishes. The impromptu, discursive quality that disfigures a novel adds a certain disarming charm to the letters.

Yet if each letter accurately reflects Simms' immediate mood, any one letter must be used with caution as reflecting either the writer or the whole man. He was not, as William P. Trent in his sermonizing biography portrayed him, either simple or simple-minded; he was instead mercurial, volatile, inconsistent, sometimes self-contradictory, and almost infinitely complex. A "high pressure steamboat" man, he had enormous mental vigor. He shot forth ideas (often sound, occasionally quixotic, but always provocative) as naturally

1

and as forcefully as a whale spouts; he wrote over eighty books and edited a baker's dozen or so of magazines; he stimulated other men to write and to publish; he was, through Northern friends and visits, a literary link between the two regions. Simms fully deserves Jay B. Hubbell's characterization of him as "the central figure in the literature of the Old South,"[2] and Vernon L. Parrington's statement that he was "the most interesting and virile figure" among ante-bellum Southern writers.[3]

A few of his letters are in the nature of brief auto-biographies. These amplify without greatly changing the known facts of his life, although they do correct many prevalent misconceptions based on errors in Trent's biography. William Gilmore Simms, Junior, was born in Charleston, April 17, 1806, of well-to-do parents. Two years later his mother died in childbirth; the infant died; and his father, already financially beset, declared that for him Charleston was only a place of tombs, and emigrated to Mississippi, to the region then known as the Southwest. With characteristic exaggeration Simms later said that his father had become bankrupt, but he left behind his infant son, 569 acres of land, two town houses, and over a score of slaves— ample support for young William and the maternal grand-mother with whom he lived.

(The mature Simms wrote disparagingly of the public and private schools he attended, and claimed that he was self-educated. Both statements have truth in them, but very few schools would be likely to satisfy a precocious boy who read omnivorously and began writing verses, according to his own account, when he was eight. In some way he learned enough that in his teens he was translating from four languages, publishing Byronic poems in local news-papers, and acquiring a wide if somewhat erratic knowledge of history and literature.

(At ten he was the principal in a dramatic trial. His grandmother had promised to send the boy to his father, but she refused to do so. The matter was taken to court. After listening to arguments on each side by locally noted orators, the judges left the decision to the boy. Gilmore decided to remain in Charleston.

It was a decision that in later life he sometimes regretted.

It intensified his sense of loneliness by isolating him from his paternal relatives, thus increasing his dependence on the imaginary world he created within his mind—a dependence that grew and burgeoned when his economical grandmother apprenticed him to a druggist, in the hope that he would become a doctor. Ultimately the decision committed him to Charleston, to South Carolina, and to literature.

There were chances to revoke the decision, most notably when Sims at the age of eighteen spent nearly a year with his father. The two rode together over the unsettled, untamed frontier. The boy met hunters, boatmen, Indians, border bandits, and venturesome farmers; he saw firsthand a raw yet romantic way of life. His father, wanting him to stay, promised a life of action and the possibility of a successful political career. Again Simms refused. He returned to Charleston to study law, edit magazines and at his own expense publish several volumes of poetry, and, perhaps most important in his own view, to marry.

This frontier visit brought out and intensified the essential dichotomy in Simms' character. By returning to Charleston he deliberately gave up a life of action, but he never got over its enticements. Possibly in South Carolina he might have combined literature and politics, but he invariably allied himself either with unpopular causes or with losing factions. In the Nullification Controversy of the early 1830s, Simms as a newspaper editor took a prominent and vehement part, against Calhoun and the Nullifiers. As a leader of the Unionist and States Rights Party, he took what seemed to him a clear, logical, defensible position: a state was paramount and had the right to secede, but as long as it remained in the Union it had no right to nullify federal laws.

Emotions, not logic, prevailed. On one occasion, Simms was almost attacked by a mob, but by his personal bravery he won admiration enough that he was unharmed and his printing presses undamaged. Psychically he did not escape unhurt. The Nullification Controversy increased his arrogant imperiousness and at the same time gave him a sense of being persecuted. Looking backward in 1844, he wrote to a young newspaper editor: "my birthplace is still the most reluctant community in the country to acknowledge my claims; and I walk the streets of my native city, very much as if I were a stranger. . . . I was of a rash and headlong disposition—soon roused, wanton sometimes in my vengeance—saying things recklessly—smiting sorely, I am now disposed to think, for no better reason than because I felt I could smite sorely."[4]

Any person who reads the frequent reviews and notices in Charleston newspapers and magazines is likely to feel that Simms was looking through the wrong end of a telescope. The best-known local critic, Hugh Swinton Legaré, had praised his verse; the local newspaper notices lauded both the writer and his achievement. But Simms felt with some justice that by being removed from the publishing centers he failed to gain the recognition due him and that he lost many advantageous opportunities for publishing; with less justice, he extended this until he felt that his city and state were inclined to disregard or actively to persecute him. Also, he was over-eager for praise. He frequently characterized as cold or feeble or unfavorable reviews that to less prejudiced eyes seem warm and generous and often just.

Disasters and tragic experiences in 1830-32 forced him into active professional writing. During this period his father, his grandmother, and his wife died. Simms, grief-stricken and almost distraught, was left with only an infant daughter who had to be cared for by maternal relatives; and his newspaper failed, leaving a heavy debt that troubled him for years. In the summer of 1832 he collected his manuscripts and set out for the North. By that time he had published five books of verse, one of them in England, but he was known mainly as an editor rather than as a writer.

His next work was a book-length poem, but it was issued by Harper's and it won favorable attention from William Cullen Bryant and lesser-known critics, and in England from the poet Thomas Campbell. Before it appeared, he had made friendships that were to endure for life with Bryant and with the Scottish-born dramatist, poet, and business man James Lawson. He and Lawson had corresponded earlier; the first letter in this collection, dated July 16, 1830, is to Lawson, and several of the latest ones (April-May 1870) are to Bryant and Lawson. On other trips he became friendly with such writers and editors as John Pendleton Kennedy, James K. Paulding, Robert Montgomery Bird, George Henry Boker, Cornelius Mathews, Evert and George Duyckinck, and, somewhat briefly, Edgar Allan Poe. The roster of his

literary friends, acquaintances, and enemies includes practi-
cally all the Knickerbocker, Philadelphia, Southern, and
Western writers of the period, with one notable exception:
Walt Whitman is not even mentioned in the extant letters.

His relations with the New England writers were tenu-
ous. In his early years he has rather half-hearted praise for
Emerson and Longfellow, and he admitted some indebtedness
to Hawthorne, but by 1845 he was taking delight in "pep-
pering Yankeedom" in his political articles and in his literary
notices. He was loyal to his New York friends; he was
jealous of the New England critics with their smug arrogance
and steady puffing of their neighbors; he felt that his own
work was unfairly treated; most of all, he disliked Massachusetts' abolitionism. Yet Simms tried, in the main successfully, to make his literary evaluations objective; some
of his best and most laudatory reviews of New England
writers were published in 1855-60.

These mixed feelings developed gradually. In 1833 he
published his first novel, *Martin Faber;* for the next decade
he concentrated so intensely on writing that he published
twelve full-length novels, two collections of tales, and one
of poems. Among his novels of this period are such well-
known works as *The Yemassee, The Partisan, Richard
Hurdis,* and *The Kinsmen.* In addition he contributed stories,
articles, reviews, and poems in a seemingly endless stream
to annuals, magazines, and newspapers. The sheer bulk of
this miscellaneous work is astounding: in one month Simms
wrote over fifty literary reviews and notices for a Charleston
paper, and somewhat later he wrote fifty-four reviews for
one issue of the *Southern Quarterly Review.*[5] He also sent
back to South Carolina newspapers lengthy reports on his
travels, and kept up a voluminous correspondence.

Although he sometimes denied it, his work suffered quali-
tatively from this staggering over-production. His closest
friend in South Carolina, James Henry Hammond, once
wrote that he had not come to Simms' house because "I
would not intrude upon your heavy labors there. . . . If
you were hewing granite to build yourself a monument as
you might do—'aere perennius,' I could admire if I did not
approve; but to be straining unremittingly, every nerve and
sinew to collect and polish pebbles that the waves of time
must soon overwhelm and absorb again into her vast obliv-

ious sea, is awful to contemplate."[6] Although he desired fame in his own lifetime and afterward, Simms apparently never admitted to himself the justice of such criticism. Instead, he held to the often-stated belief that "fame does not so much follow polish and refinement as Genius—not so much grace and correct delineation as a bold adventurous thought."[7] In addition, there was in him a compulsion to write: "If I wander, I muse; if I muse, I compose; if I compose, I am feverish, 'till I can grasp the pen and make the record."[8]

He early developed a clear, sinewy, serviceable style, but he never conquered his tendency toward discursiveness. Perhaps more important, he never reconciled his natural bent toward realism and his liking for stories of adventurous action. In addition, Simms was intellectually restless. He virtually abandoned fiction in favor of editing magazines and writing history, geography, and biographies. In the 1840s, also, his interest in politics revived. He served one term in the state legislature and was almost elected Lieutenant-Governor; he desired a high office or a diplomatic or consular post, but characteristically he refused to campaign or to work effectively for these positions. There was another obvious defect, which his friend Hammond stated explicitly: "what personal causes have prevented your elevation? . . . You want the art of concealing your superiority. Even though you may not intend or desire it, you make it palpable to every one you come in contact with."[9] Simms admitted this, but he made little or no effort to temper his imperiousness or diplomatically to phrase his dogmatic judgments.

Although he became a fiery secessionist, Simms was locally allied once more with a losing faction. The Hammonds were not popular; they were anti-Calhoun; they could help Simms but little. In fact, the many letters between them indicate that Simms was more effective in giving help than the Hammonds were. Yet, again characteristically, it never occurred to Simms to abandon his friends because they were out of favor.

He was even more devoted to his family. In 1836 he married Chevillette Roach, the only child of a well-to-do plantation owner. From the time of his marriage Simms spent his winters at Woodlands, halfway between Charleston and Augusta, and many of his letters reveal his interest in agricultural experiments and his pleasure in hunting and fishing. Practically every personal letter tells something about his children. He fathered fifteen; he buried nine. The most tragic and emotion-charged letters in these volumes are those telling of the deaths of his children, and in 1863 of his wife. These disasters caused him to write that he was "a man marked for the scourge."[10]

Neither personal tragedy nor what he considered a lack of proper recognition stopped him from writing. In 1852 he published his best novel, *The Sword and the Distaff* (later he changed the title to *Woodcraft*), and the following year he began revising his novels for a collected edition, with illustrations by F. O. C. Darley.

His interest in politics, his belief in the goodness of slavery, and his unwavering faith in the rightness of his own convictions led in 1856 to a strange and almost disastrous contretemps. He had agreed to lecture in the North. Instead of choosing a literary topic he gave as his first lecture, "South Carolina in the Revolution." But he included a liberal amount of contemporary material, beginning with an intemperate attack upon Senator Sumner of Massachusetts. Originally he had intended for the lectures to "establish better relations between the North and the South"; somehow and with poor judgment he decided that it was his "mission" to set the North straight, thus "disabusing them of those errors which were leading them on to ruin; and my own blood was in a ferment." In this mood he went forth "to preach"—or, as Hammond charged, "to take the North by the nose, in its state of highest excitement and utmost exasperation and to subdue [it] to your will by rhetoric and argument." Although Simms claimed that his audiences "howled under the arguments they could not answer," the Northerners won the contest simply by staying away from his lectures. Simms cancelled the lecture tour, and gave the money he had already earned to charity.[11]

After this episode and indeeed before it, Simms was ready for South Carolina to secede. Although refusing to be an avowed candidate, he vainly desired in 1860 to be elected a delegate to the South Carolina "Secession Convention." His plan was simple and clear-cut. "If elected, I shall aim at but a single object—to separate from a Confederacy in which we are otherwise doom'd to destruction."[12] He advised his New York friend James Lawson to move South, assuring him that "there will be no war. A war would destroy the whole confederacy of the North, and make that of the South supreme."[13]

By the end of 1860 he had changed his mind. War, he decided, was inevitable. But he was too old and too ill physically to take an active part in the fighting; he could only remain at Woodlands "like a bear with a sore head, and chained to the stake. I chafe, and roar and rage, but can do nothing."[14] Yet he could and did write long, detailed letters about the coastal defenses of Charleston, and many of his suggestions were effectively. employed by army leaders. Always of an excitable temperament, he justified one letter by declaring that "I am sleepless . . . and must write."[15] There seeemd to him, also, obvious defects in the South Carolina and the Confederate governments, but his practical, sensible advice to political friends had no effect. The immediately pressing problems so engrossed him that he wrote to Paul Hamilton Hayne, "My heart is too full of anxiety to suffer me to write, and though I have a contract for some two hundred dollars worth of prose, I find myself unable to divert my thoughts from the crisis in which the country trembles in suspense. What I write is in a spasm, a single burst of passion,—hope, or scorn, or rage, or exultation."

He came out of the war a widower, destitute, his oldest son severely wounded and sick, his home burned, his library destroyed. He was humbled and chastened, but he was not personally defeated. The Simms of the post-war years seems altogether admirable. For a pittance he edited and wrote for struggling Southern newspapers; he worked vigorously toward making Woodlands as self-sufficient as a plantation could be; he pocketed his pride, journeyed to New York, and agreed to write for small magazines that could pay him pitiably little. He renewed old friendships with Lawson and Duyckinck, and later with Bryant; he doled out carefully to needy persons (including Timrod) the money which generous Northern friends sent to him.

He was no longer interested in fame or recognition. He desired only to support his family in meager comfort, and he wrote his children pathetically that "Your father will divide himself among you, and so long as his poor brains can be turned to profit, he will use them for your good."[17] Among other works he edited an anthology, *War Poetry of the South;* amazingly, with this and other hack work, he produced an interesting, creditable romance (*Voltmeier, or The Mountain Man;* never published in book form) and one of the finest tall tales ever written by a Southern humorist, "How Sharp Snaffles Got His Capital and His Wife." Literally he forced himself to work, for he was sick, probably with cancer, throughout these years. He died on June 11, 1870.

In an excellently-written, provocative Introduction to the *Letters,* Donald Davidson surveys the contemporary neglect of Simms' work, and suggests, perhaps too enthusiastically, that twelve or fifteen of his books should be made available in modern reprints. More than most writers, Simms needs to be carefully winnowed. From his nineteen books of verse a careful editor could select a small volume of good and sometimes distinguished poems; from the mass of his tales and stories, an even better book could be put together. The historical, political, and even the literary articles were hastily written; quite a few—notably the critique on James Fenimore Cooper—are worth salvaging. Simms as romancer and novelist is represented in current publications only by the earlier, sometimes powerful, but rather chaotic *Yemassee.* The seven novels of the Revolution have better stuff in them: they have an over-abundance of adventure, wild conflict, and historical digression, but they testify convincingly that war degrades rather than ennobles and that a powerful writer can sometimes compensate for his defects. The quieter concluding novel, *Woodcraft,* reveals Simms at his best; more than any other of his works, with the possible exception of *Border Beagles,* it deserves to be reprinted and to be read.

He needed the curb of a strict art-form, but he wrote in a period that encouraged looseness and diffuseness. This suited his own restless, prolific mind: even late in life, he noted, "I find it much easier to invent a new story than to repair the defects of an old one."[18] Ultimately this inability to discipline his mind and his work makes the epitaph he suggested for himself only too just and true: "Here lies one who, after a reasonably long life, distinguished chiefly by unceasing labors, has left all his better works undone."

Chapter II

On Novels and Novelists

It is natural that Simms' best and most influential criticism deals with fiction. Although he sometimes expressed distrust of that medium and fancied his true forte was as poet or dramatist, he was most at home writing or writing about prose fiction. He had so many other interests that for almost a decade (1842-51) he neglected fiction to concentrate heavily on writing history, geography, and especially biography; he devoted an inordinate amount of time and thought to politics, military strategy, and the defense of slavery; he yielded easily to requests for occasional poems and orations; he edited too many impecunious magazines and filled far too many of their pages with hasty hack work.

There were good and possibly quite valid reasons for all this activity. He was a professional man of letters living in Charleston or on his father-in-law's plantation "Woodlands:" that is, at a far remove from the center of profitable literary and publishing activities, yet largely dependent on that activity for a livelihood. It is to this necessity rather than to other interests that C. Hugh Holman attributes "Simms's virtual abandoning" of fiction between 1842 and 1850: the writing of novels was no longer profitable because of "the devastating effect on American fiction of the [continuing] Panic of 1837, the pirating of English popular novels and the development of the 'mammoth weeklies' and the 'cheap book' publishers."[1] Simms frequently and bitterly noted how the sales of his novels had declined. Thus in 1841 he wrote that "Irving now writes almost wholly for magazines and Cooper and myself are almost the only persons whose novels are printed—certainly, we are almost the only persons who hope to get anything from them. From England we get nothing. In this country an Edition now instead of 4 or 5,000 copies, is scarce 2,000. My Damsel of Darien [1839] was 3,000. My Kinsmen [1841] not more than 2,000; and it is seldom now that the demand for novels carries them to a 2d Edition. . . . Nothing, in short, but the great popularity of an author will secure the publication of a novel now."[2]

These conditions led his friend and publisher Mathew Carey to advise Simms to stop writing novels. Partly influenced by economic conditions but even more by a general distrust of the value of fiction, his friends James H. Hammond and Benjamin F. Perry counselled him to write only histories and biographies. Simms yielded to what he must have regarded as necessity, but by 1850 he was convinced that he had been wrong to do so. Except for the biography of Francis Marion, the sales of these books had been disappointing, and his history of South Carolina "did not yield me as much money as I have earned in three nights, penning legends for the Annuals."[3] Perhaps equally important was his considered belief that "the works that make fame are works which admit of the exercises of originality, and chiefly belong to the imaginative faculty."

This included all forms of creative writing, but as one pertinent illustration he noted that "Boccaccio undervalued his stories and built upon his treatises. The last are forgotten and he lives by the former."[4] Even more relevant is the fact that when he mentions Homer and Aeschylus, he is not talking of practitioners of an alien craft, but as in a sense his own direct literary ancestors. Like many of his contemporaries, Simms attempted to draw a sharp line of demarcation between the novel and the romance. Most of his own works, he wrote emphatically to E. A. Duyckinck, "are *romances*, not novels," and therefore "involve sundry of the elements of heroic poetry."[5]

He developed this theme at some length in the 1853 Preface to the revised *Yemassee*. He demanded that critics recognize the distinction and judge the book by the "standards which have governed me in its composition."[6] These standards were reasonably clear in his own mind: "The Modern Romance is the substitute which the people of the present day offer for the epic. The form is changed; the matter is very much the same; at all events, it differs much more seriously from the English novel than it does from the epic and the drama." The reader who employs Fielding and Richardson as his touchstones can never satisfactorily read *Ivanhoe*, for the domestic novel deals with ordinary characters in ordinary conditions of society; the romance, differing in material even more than in mode, "is of loftier origin than the Novel. It approximates the poem. It may be described as an amalgam of the two. It is only with those who are apt to insist upon poetry as verse, and to confound rhyme with poetry, that the resemblance is unapparent."

The standards of the romance are similar to those of the epic, and to these the writer is "required religiously to confine himself." Simms' definition may seem inadequate both for the epic and the romance, but he explained frankly what he was trying to do: The romance as he wrote it "invests individuals with an absorbing interest—it hurries them rapidly through crowding and exacting events, in a narrow space of time—it requires the same unities of plan, of purpose, and harmony of parts, and it seeks for its adventures among the wild and wonderful."

This distinction was clear-cut, but its application was not always easy. Sometimes he described his stories of the Revolution as novels, sometimes as romances; at least one of them, *Eutaw*, was "at once a novel of society and a romance."[7] For him this was a remarkable concession. Ordinarily he thought poorly of domestic novels, "a very inferior school of writings," because the "imagination can have little play. The exercise of the creative faculty is almost entirely denied."[8] As a result, the author must depend on "analysis of minute shades of character," and description of tame social events. Simms preferred works that were "imaginative, passionate, metaphysical"; he preferred, as a general rule, "to give a story of events, rather than of persons."[9]

Although he felt that readers preferred action to analysis and tended (except in the psychological novel) to agree with them, he recognized that "success in drawing character" was "one of the most important requisites in modern romance and novel writing."[10] He semi-apologizes for stopping the action in *Beauchampe* (p. 46) to give "proper characterization," but defends himself (unnecessarily, it would seem) on the ground that the "novel only answers half its uses when we confine it to the simple delineation of events, however ingenious and interesting." In *Confession*, the story depended almost wholly on an analysis of the passions, of "the heart in some of its obliquities and perversities"; Simms admitted in the Preface to the second edition that he had revised the work "with many misgivings." It lacked variety, color, incident; it appealed to the brain rather than to the blood. He did not expect it to be popular, for success of this kind "is rarely possible in any work of fiction where events, which naturally speak for themselves, are mostly rejected from use."[11]

In general, he preferred simply that his characters be portrayed truthfully, as the author had known similar persons in life, with their inconsistencies as well as their basic governing attributes.[12] This emphasis on actuality extended to conversation: R. M. Bird in *The Infidel* was wrong aesthetically and realistically in letting his "Cavaliers all speak the same language."[13] With certain historical personages the author was closely bound, and Simms notes, for example, that General Marion in *Mellichampe* is "correct to the very letter of the written history."[14] The story of Captain Barsfield's conversion to Toryism "is not less so," although it is based on tradition rather than records; Simms notes its "close resemblance to the recorded history" of another and more famous Southern loyalist. The romancer also had the right to transpose incidents from the life of a known character to that of a fictional one, as Simms did when he borrowed freely from the career of Col. Isaac Hayne to round out his portrait of Col. Walton.[15] One could likewise transpose incidents, as he did when he described the "destruction of the mansion-house at 'Piney Grove' by Major Singleton . . . the means employed to effect this object [fire-bearing arrows supplied by the owner's daughter], will be recognized by the readers of Carolina history, and the lover of female patriotism, as of true occurrence in every point of view; the names of persons alone being altered, and a slight variation made in the locality."[16]

He did not always bother with even a slight disguise, but mingled his fictional character freely with historical ones, as he openly declared, again typically, in *Katharine Walton*: "The scenes of this story, which occur in Charleston, were mostly of real occurrence, as the parties were mostly real and well-known persons." In the same book Simms describes a precipitate marriage in which the groom held a pistol in his hand throughout the ceremony, but he apparently feared this incident might seem unreal, for he assures the reader that the marriage "did actually take place, under these very circumstances, and between these very parties," and that the officiating minister had recorded all the particulars.

Sometimes he transposed equally unlikely incidents from his own personal knowledge, especially from his experiences on the frontier; thus, after describing how an outlaw escaped by floating down an Alabama river on a bag of cotton, Simms added a footnote: "This is a fact; such a mode of escape would not readily suggest itself to a romancer's invention, but it did to that of a very great rogue."[17]

Incidents from history, legend, or personal knowledge could be used effectively provided they were used in such a way as to add verisimilitude to the story. But an accumulation of facts, even though each might in itself be true, was not enough to prove a case. This was one fundamental error that Harriet Beecher Stowe had made in *Uncle Tom's Cabin*. Many of her isolated facts were true, yet the novel was "a wholesale lie." She claimed that her work was based on fact, but this was not enough: "Admit all her statements to be true, and they prove nothing. Her facts may be susceptible of proof, while her inferences are wholly false."[18] The romancer could use uncharacteristic or isolated facts to advantage because they are rare but possible; the writer of social protest could not. Mrs. Stowe had ignorantly confused the *genres*, so that *Uncle Tom's Cabin* was as deficient artistically as it was sociologically: "The structure of the romance, to which class of writings Mrs. Stowe's story belongs, is one that demands extraordinary events. In this respect it transcends the privileges of the ordinary novel of society. The interest is maintained by startling incidents, and these require constantly to rise in their excitements in order to produce the proper effects. The standards, measurably, are those of the drama. Scene follows scene; act, act; event crowds upon the heels of events; one incident prepares the way for another still more imposing, till the gradually swelling spectacle finds its *denouement* in an event of such magnitude and importance to the parties, as leaves it beyond the power of the dramatist to go further."[19] To Simms' mind, although she wrote with passion and power, Mrs. Stowe's novel was deficient as "art and argument."

Yet his concern with strict artistry was limited. In most novels he is the omniscient author who does not hesitate to tell what is or is not true, what must or must not be supposed; to announce bluntly in the middle of a chapter that "we must now return" to another group of characters; or naively to assure the reader that he can listen in on secret conferences, in which he will remain unseen to the participants.[20] Occasionally he used the device of the fictional narrator and let the supposed speaker present the story, usually although not completely according to his own developing knowledge, as in *Confession;* but in *Richard Hurdis* he endows his narrator with practically total recall as to the exact words of long conversations. Simms attempted to justify the method in a Preface written eighteen years after its first publication: "It will be seen that there is a peculiarity in the arrangement of the story. The hero tells, not only what he himself performed, but supplies the events, even as they occur, which he yet derives from the report of others. Though quite unusual, the plan is yet strictly within the proprieties of art. The reader can readily be made to comprehend that the hero writes after a lapse of time, in which he had supplied himself with the necessary details, filling up the gaps in his own experience. I have persuaded myself that something is gained by such a progress, in the more energetic, direct and dramatic character of the story; and the rapidity of the action is a necessary result, from the exclusion of all circuitous narrative. The hero and author, under the plan, become identical."[21] To the modern reader, however, Simms appears to have sacrificed whatever advantages there may be in the first person narrator, without any compensations. There is rather less awkwardness in his transitions when he is himself the omniscient author.

When he provided direct historical information in an Introduction or even as part of the first chapter, the material seems relevant and properly placed. But he did not hesitate to interrupt the action in order to interpolate historical mat-

ter, without any attempt to weave it into the story, or
hesitate to include a lengthy and argumentative footnote in
order to set a somewhat irrelevant record straight.[22]

Yet the writer of historical romances was not a historian.
He should be factually accurate and he should have as much
personal knowledge as possible; thus Simms wrote that he
could not complete *The Yemassee* "until I have in *pro. per.*
gone over the ground of the story, and become acquainted
with its localities."[23] But the subject must have a "certain
degree of obscurity," and the events "must be such as will
admit of the full exercise of the great characteristic of genius—
imagination. He must be free to conceive and to invent—to
create and to endow;—without any dread of crossing the
confines of ordinary truth, and of such history as may be
found in undisputed records. His material must be of such a
kind as to leave him without danger of rebuke for impropriety; and the only laws and criteria against which he must
provide, must be those of good taste and probability, with
such other standards as he himself sets up in his progress,
as gauges by which to work, himself, and by which others
are to judge of his performances. When we are told that a
history is too fresh for fiction, it is because of this danger
that it is so. When it is objected that America is too young
for the production of a national literature, it is chiefly because
of this difficulty, which fetters and defies domestic invention.
Genius dare not take liberties with a history so well known,
and approaches her task with a cautious apprehensiveness
which is inconsistent with her noblest executions."[24]

Both the regular historian and the romancer needed first
of all to be an artist, so that readers would feel that the
historical "dry-bones were once covered with flesh." To a
large degree, history is informed conjecture; it is raw material
to be handled honestly and scrupulously, but "the chief
value of history consists in its proper employment for the
purposes of art. . . . It is by such artists, indeed, that nations
live."[25] For a major defect with history is that as written
it is "the history rather of princes than of people,"[26] and it
pays little or no attention to social customs and manners,
ordinary human beings, and minor events: the historical
romance "supplies those details which the latter, unwisely as
we think, but too commonly, holds beneath her regard."[27]

It was the function of the romancer to fill in the gaps left by the formal historian. This liberty did not extend to distortion of the material. His comment on *The Yemassee* illustrates the limitations he imposed on himself: "It is needless to add that the historical events are strictly true." But the romancer could make freer use of imagination, invention, and design.

Without disparaging history, he valued most "the free use which the imaginative mind may make of that which is unknown, fragmentary and in ruins—the *debris* of history, and not the perfect fragment."[28] The imagination was all-powerful and all-important, and it derived at least in part from the intuition. It came before invention and design; it could be shaped but not wholly controlled by conscious discipline. Simms apparently believed, contrary to his own practice, that the main work of the imagination should be complete before a particular work was begun; he advised his younger friend and fellow-novelist John Esten Cooke to "Give yourself time enough to contemplate your ground and materials fully, so as to *design* with a better grasp of the *absolute* in your subject. It is thus that it always shows itself arbitrarily fixed in its object. It must go in one direction—speak in one character—pursue one outline, and has no choice. The imagination, if not a will itself, seems to work under a will which is imperative as fate, and allows it no caprices. It is the fancy which wanders and has a frequent choice."[29]

Here and elsewhere (notably in a review of Bulwer's work) Simms equates the imagination with the creative faculty; whereas fancy equates with the decorative ornamental faculty: "Imagination may be described as the architect who designs the noble temple . . . fancy, that subordinate artist who lays out the grounds below."[30]

Although more limited, the function of invention was equally important. No man could be a first-rate novelist who did not have in a high degree the "constructive faculty"; it was James Fenimore Cooper's major weakness that he "seems to exercise none of his genius in the invention of his fable. There is none of that careful grouping of means to ends, and all, to the one end of the denouement, which so remarkably distinguished the genius of Scott."[31] Instead, Cooper relied on the "spirit and success of certain scenes," disregarding the fact that in the romance "all the standards are dramatic," and that "the perfecting of the wondrous whole—the admirable adaptation of means to ends—the fitness of parts—the propriety of the action—the employment of the right materials,—and the fine architectural proportions of the fabric,—these are the essentials which determine the claim of the writer to be the BUILDER."

Through invention, then, the author provided a continuous, harmonious action. Simms objected to writing short stories because in them "no room is allowed you for the development of character, you have to rely chiefly on incident and this tasks invention to the uttermost."[32] He believed, rather, that incidents should grow out of the development of character.

As some of the preceding quotations suggest, design has to do with the over-all pattern of the story, rather than with artistry. In the Preface to *Mellichampe*, Simms admitted that critics of *The Partisan* had been justified in calling it crude and unfinished; it was rapidly prepared, and "the finish of art can only be claimed by a people with whom art is a leading object." But when objection was made "simply to the story, *as a story*," Simms at once defended the novel, although he confessed that the "design may have been unhappy, and in that my error may have lain."[33] Perhaps Simms is half-way admitting here that in the Revolutionary stories he had thrown in too much undigested history and given too much attention to military strategy and tactics. When Simms was revising his work for the collected edition, J. H. Hammond advised him to "use the knife freely and cut out every thing that impedes the action. I used even as a boy to curse Scott for his long twaddling scenes and you must not blame me if I say that you have caught that failing from him . . . the writer who has fine things to say must weave them so closely into his very framework that they will appear to belong necessarily to the tale."[34]

In theory Simms agreed fully with Hammond. He noted that Cooper often rode his intellectual hobbies too hard, to the disquiet of his readers,[35] and that Ainsworth, lacking design, depended on the accumulation of details to hold interest.[36] Fiction required both more invention and a more elaborate treatment than non-fiction; it must be shaped "with proper care, with a becoming purpose, and under a severer, sublimer design."[37] To a young writer he indicated clearly the defects caused by faulty design: "You have too many persons to manage. You cannot group them into consistent and condensed action. You bring forward too prominently persons who do not help on the action, and several of the early scenes which delay the reader have no obvious connection with the catastrophes."[38]

He admitted freely his own similar errors, but he attributed them in part to the indifference of American readers to careful artistry, and in part to his own impetuosity of temperament and consequent over-hasty writing. Of *Beauchampe* he wrote to his friend B. F. Perry that "The work was written *stans pede in uno*, goon like, literally, as fast as pen could fly over paper,—pretty much as I write to you now. A mode not very favorable to a work of permanent merit, but particularly suited to a temperament like mine."[39]

Possibly as a rationalization of his own defects, Simms tended to set a low value on artistry. The essential qualities, the best proofs of originality, were "passion or power";[40] if a writer had these, he could safely disregard the time-consuming niceties: "fame does not so much follow polish and refinement as Genius—not so much grace and correct delineation as a bold adventurous thought."[41] Yet the mercurial Simms—though always ready to lash out at publishers, editors, and critics, and to advise that a literary work might better be tried on the cook—had many moments of uneasiness. When he was not defending himself, he was capable, typically, of confessing to N. B. Tucker that "I do not know that I should desire you to read the things which I have sent you. I feel all their feeblenesses and crudenesses. They were written most of them at an extremely early age, and under the pressure of necessities which left me too careless of any but present and momentary considerations. You will find them wanting in symmetry and finish, and grossly disfigured by errors of taste and judgment." But in them, he hoped, Tucker would find "proofs of original force, native character, and some imagination."[42]

If Simms was inconsistent about the need for artistry and about his accomplishment, he was steadily consistent about morality in literature. Any work of the imagination must be ultimately useful, in the "most elevated meaning" of that word, for it must "answer to our want as human beings, of mixed earth and spirit: having a human necessity before us which however lowly, is the absolute essential to any higher or more hopeful condition."[43] So Bulwer makes a common but unwholesome error when he places the ideal in opposition to the real; Simms, with rather more grasp of good sense than of philosophy, argued that this placed the ideal beyond the reach of men, whereas the moral purpose of art should be attainable, for "the ideal is nothing more than the possible real. . . . To show the real as it is, is the subordinate but preliminary task of genius. It is the holding the mirror up to the common nature. To contrast with this the image of the real, such as it may become, is the holding the mirror up to the universal nature." In this, Simms roundly declared, "consists the morals of art; writers like Shelley and Bulwer might think otherwise, but Homer, Dante, Shakspeare, and Milton never made this error."[44]

One function of genius is to lead "people out of the bondage of the present." For this exalted and frequently agonizing task, prose fiction was not a satisfactory medium: "The mere business of novel-writing, as it is ordinarily conducted, is about the humblest way in which genius can employ itself."[45] Even so, the novel could be useful, for it is of value in the highest sense when it "ministers to morals, to mankind, and to society."[46]

This did not require sermonizing, or pointing a moral. The writer must always keep in mind that we do not take up a poem or novel "in the same frame of mind with which we approach a volume of sermons." The preacher attempts to inculcate moral and religious truth, but the business of the novelist is simply to be truthful. Since human nature is seldom wholly good or bad, "a character either wholly good or bad never yet entered into the imagination of the dramatist or novelist." It is the "mixt" character that the novelist deals with, and if he presents a true picture, "the author has succeeded—and the reader or critic may cavil, if he please, about the 'cakes and ale'."[47]

Simms returned to this theme time and again, perhaps nowhere more clearly than in a review, "Modern Prose

Fiction": "As truthfulness is never without its moral, and as the great end of the artist is the approximation of all his fiction to a seeming truth, so unavoidably he inculcates a moral whenever he tells a story." It does not follow that all authors are moral, for many of them did not aim at truthfulness at all; but any author who deserved to be called an artist would be moral in proportion as he succeeded in being truthful.[48]

When his own work was attacked as low, vulgar, and immoral, Simms presented as a personal defense the same arguments he had presented generally. Reviewers who had objected to the "preponderance of low and vulgar personages" in *The Partisan* had not properly understood the function of the romancer. He was not presenting the equivalent of a rosy-hued fairy tale, or an account of "inane perfectibility." He claimed for himself a realistic purpose: "My object usually has been to adhere, as closely as possible, to the features and the attributes of real life, as it is to be found in the precise scene, and under the governing circumstances—some of them extraordinary and romantic, because new—in which my narrative has followed it." Certain portraits in his novels might not be pleasing to some readers, but Simms was persuaded that in them he had "done mankind no injustice."[49]

When the publication of "[Caloya; or] The Loves of the Driver" in the *Magnolia* brought forth horrified but nasty and unfounded objections, Simms responded vigorously to the attack, protesting that in his story there was nothing "that can, in the slightest degree, prove hurtful to the delicacy of the purest mind." He had not made vice beautiful or attractive, or virtue ugly. True, it was "a tale of low life—very low life," but there was nothing salacious or prurient in it. So many people were afflicted with "mock modesty" that authors were reluctant "to call things by their proper names. We dare not speak of legs, or thighs, in the presence of many very nice ladies."[50] He adds that if Shakspeare were writing *The Merry Wives* for nineteenth century readers, certain words would be objected to, but the real evil would be in the mind of that person who objected to the correct use of an exact word; even Shakspeare would have "to soften one of the words used into 'female dog,' 'feminine dog,' or something equally inoffensive and equally stupid; but while it would be perfectly moral to say 'bitch' where the sense called for it, it would be a proof of an immodest thought, in the mind of the the speaker, who should say 'female dog'!"[51]

This plea for the use of "appropriate language" was a minor part of his defense. He felt that he had re-created characters as he had known them in real life; that moral justice had been allowed to triumph by "natural and ordinary" means; and that the Indian woman in his story embodied a high order of morality. He had presented strong passions, but he had not falsified them; so in earlier days had many of the Biblical writers, and after them Homer, Shakspeare, Massinger, Scott, and Byron: In fact, the "whole tribe of great names, employ the deadly sins of man, as so many foils to his living virtues and whether he falls or triumphs, the end of the moralist is attained, if he takes care to speak the truth, the whole truth and nothing but the truth! In this, in fact, lies the whole secret of his art. *A writer is moral only in proportion to his truthfulness.*"[52]

This did not mean that the author, especially the romancer, was bound by the literal fact. As Alexander Cowie has indicated, Simms had read Aristotle's *Poetics* to good purpose, and conformed to the Aristotelian dictum that a "likely impossibility is preferable to an unconvincing possibility."[53] Although he praised its "fearlessness and ingenuity," he condemned Mrs. Shelley's *Frankenstein* for its "extreme violation of natural laws,"[54] and he was careful that his own Gothic effects were rationally explainable; but he never wavered from his belief that imaginative or intuitive understanding was fundamentally more truthful than historical fact or rational comprehension. Only through the skill and imagination of the artist could history be made to yield its ultimate meanings.

II

The best writer of prose fiction, in Simms' estimation, was clearly Sir Walter Scott; with the possible exception of Milton and Dryden, he was the best English writer since Shakspeare. He lacked intuitive insight, but his success in depicting characters was "the grand secret" of his pre-eminence. His one defect was in the feebleness and passivity of his heroes, in comparison with relatively minor characters, but Scott's willingness to give himself completely to his subject and to his characters redeemed what otherwise would have been fatal to a dramatic composition. Also, Scott had boldly broken away from the inferior domestic novel, so that the works of Fielding and Richardson did not provide adequate, correct, or even relevant standards by which to judge Scott's romances.[55]

He was equally outstanding in his power to impose on his material a design that carried the reader step by step, naturally and easily, with no sense of artistic impropriety or violence, until the complete story was a "harmonious achievement."[56] In his letters, articles, and books Simms made casual allusions to Scott's phrases and characters in such a way as to reveal a thorough familiarity; more important, in his criticism he constantly used Scott as a touchstone by which to judge other novelists. He was especially inclined to use *Ivanhoe* in this way, for it seemed to him "one of the most perfect specimens of the romance that we possess. . . . Impaired, however, by the single piece of mummery toward the close, which embodies the burial rites of Athelstane and his resurrection. But for this every way unbecoming episode, the romance would be nearly perfect."[57] Moreover, with it Scott had done what the romancer should always strive to do: he had changed the previously-accepted historical concept of the period.

Simms' admiration for the earlier English novelists was limited. He remembered that as a boy he "used to glow and shiver in turn" over *Pilgrim's Progress*,[58] and in *Eutaw* he presents through several chapters the way in which that book literally saved the life of an outlaw, and effected a partial if temporary regeneration of a previously ruthless desperado.[59] Parts of the *Vicar of Wakefield* threw him "into paroxysms of laughter"; Sterne, although a humorist of a superior order, erred in making a single character responsible for the "whole interest of his story"; Defoe and Swift, masters in handling detail, helped bring about the "natural merging" of the drama with prose fiction.[60] But he seems to have thought more highly of Fielding and Smollett, "English masters of comic fiction," as humorists than as novelists: they were working directly in the tradition of Chaucer, with the grafting on of some "foreign attributes." This means that their humor "grew naturally out of the situation . . . the spontaneous effusion of a faculty in themselves, and in the character and the event upon which they were engaged." They did not rely on quaintness of phraseology, odd nomenclature, or cunning contrivances, but allowed their humor simply to grow out of life as they knew it.[61]

Scott shared this ability, but in him humor was tributary, "always subservient to the tragedy—a foil rather than a constituent." Dickens also had a genuine sense of humor, but one too frequently distorted; if Chaucer had written modern prose narratives "like those of Mr. Dickens," they would have been constructed "with better plots, less extravagance, and something less of the pathetic." But Dickens, like Chaucer, had as a prominent part of his genius "that pliancy of mood, for example, which we call mental flexibility, and which enables him to go out of himself, to forget himself, to forget his favorite thoughts and fancies, and to throw all the strength of his intellect into the *dramatis personae* that grow under his hands." Homer, Shakspeare, and Scott possessed this ability; Byron and Bulwer did not, and Milton was "a kingman . . . who impressed all persons with his own nature, and made all speak after the fashion of his own soul . . . he made the world after his own models." Although admitting the superlative genius of Milton, Simms in general preferred what he called "many-sidedness" in an author.

Yet one of the most powerful immediate influences on Simms as novelist was by an intense, single-track writer. As he frankly admits in the Introduction, *Confession* belongs to "the class of works which the genius of William Godwin has made to triumph in 'Caleb Williams,' even over a perverse system." *Martin Faber* also clearly reveals the influence of Godwin. Although he was doubtful that such works could be made popular, Simms was interested both in reading and writing psychological novels about crime.

The "many-sided" author could compensate for looseness of structure in a way that the intense novelist could not. That was clearly an advantage which Charles Dickens enjoyed over William Godwin. The weaknesses of Dickens were to be found, typically, in *Bleak House*, with its "exaggeration in the portraiture" and its failure in the over-all design—a failure that Simms in several notices of Dickens' works blamed on serial publication of parts of a book, to the neglect of the unified whole.[62] Occasionally he was outdone by Dickens' carelessness: he declared roundly that if *The Haunted Man* had "been issued by an unknown writer, it woud have been generally pronounced a wretched piece of drivel."[63] He praised *Hard Times* as "very characteristic. . . . Its portraiture is mournfully true and terribly human throughout. The story is painfully pleasing; the softening features in *Hard Times* admirably contrasting with the iron of the age." But his verdict on Dickens at his best is well summed up in his comment on *David Copperfield*: "The delineation of character is inimitable in particular cases, and unexceptionable in most. The 'Child Wife' portrait is very happy, and Micawber, in his miseries, extremely so."[64]

His admiration for Thackeray was at once more limited and more complex. As editor of the *Southern Quarterly Review* he accepted and published an article describing Thackeray as the finest delineator of human nature since Fielding;[65] in the next issue, in reviewing *Pendennis*, Simms dissents sharply: Thackeray's "art is not of the highest character, and we are very far from concurring with one of our contributors, who . . . gave us a very spirited and well-written, but highly exaggerated, estimate of the genius of Thackeray."[66] Thackeray had "a wonderful faculty in minute painting—in social detail"; he had also a "keen insight into human frailties and vanities . . . stripping bare the fraud, and cant, and hypocrisy of pretentious people."[67] But this faculty was too often, as in *The Virginians*, greatly overworked: "the bad and the base—the mean and the malignant—are allotted as usual, too large a proportion of its pages."[68] This had led many readers to misunderstand Thackeray, as man and as writer. His talent was "eminently essayical," and his "art is genial. His art, in fact, is truer than his sentiments. . . . His genius is more just than his sympathies." Simms as novelist and critic liked "mixt" characters, but the cynicism of Thackeray offended one who believed that "Man is a much better animal, in his worst rags, than we are inclined to think him";[69] when Thackeray changed the "stern, simple, sublime character of Washington" to an undignified, raging, roaring, ordinary man, Simms was thoroughly infuriated.[70]

Yet his distaste for Thackeray's philosophy of life did not blind him to Thackeray's mastery in fiction of construction and design. Technically, Thackeray was a master of his craft, and Simms set a high value on any novelist who could impose an artistic design on his material. He enjoyed also Thackeray's "felicitous and peculiar vein of drollery and humor," especially in his shorter works, but he indulged himself too much in "a harsh and savage portrait of humanity." Rather oddly, but almost entirely because of what he considered faulty characterization of real people, Simms in reviewing *Henry Esmond* expressed a preference for Thackeray as a "domestic and social humourist" rather than as a writer of romances. *Henry Esmond* had many attractions for the reader, and Simms admitted that some characters were well drawn and forcible, but the exaggerated and unbalanced portrait of Sir Richard Steele and the tone of the book alike roused him to protest. He could admire Thackeray's skill, but he apparently did not in his heart either like or admire Thackeray.[71]

One of Simms' major critical essays is "Bulwer's Genius and Writings."[72] In it he gave his own definition, previously noted, of imagination and fancy, and one of his best statements on the use of the real and the ideal. The article is more critical than the title indicates: at the beginning he admits Bulwer's genius, but here as elsewhere he uses the term to include spirit, intention, characteristics, and performance, by those men who were struggling "constantly to leave the common track." Bulwer had large and various natural endowments; he thought with boldness, conceived with courage, and painted with ardor. But the genius of Bulwer had within itself two startling flaws. The first was the more serious: "a certain obliquity of the moral sense, which seems to make it impossible for him, under certain lights, to distinguish between right and wrong";[73] and with this, a boyish and vain desire to startle by vehement novelties simply for the pleasure of gratifying his own egotism. As a result, "Bulwer is rather a writer of fancy than imagination"; although credited with boldness, he is really not bold enough in his imaginative grasp of concepts—

possibly because of his weak creative powers, his deficiency of artistic imagination. Bulwer fascinated Simms, and he was highly pleased when a reviewer wrote that he had read *The Yemassee* "with a deeper interest and more unalloyed gratification than any preceding work of imagination since the *Last Days of Pompeii*";[74] he had in many short notices and reviews a sincere praise for Bulwer's accomplishments. But he was forced, somewhat reluctantly, to declare that he could not rank Bulwer "among the fathers of his time."[75]

A writer with some of Bulwer's characteristics, Benjamin D'Israeli, presented an easier critical case. He had been unjustly neglected by some English critics, notably R. H. Horne; he had not, like Scott, Carlyle, Wordsworth, Coleridge, and Bulwer, profoundly affected his age, but novels like *Coningsby* and *Venetia* had individuality and power. The neglect was primarily D'Israeli's own fault; his "endowments . . . are various and showy. He has never made the best, or even a proper, use of them."[76] Yet in spite of many faults arising mainly out of vanity and ambition, D'Israeli knew well the society that he described with a lively fancy, and he had "a power in conversational dialogue, which is not often surpassed among novel writers." To offset these virtues, "His invention is small. His mind is too versatile for that degree of concentrativeness which is required for weaving together, in harmonious connection and dependency, the intricate details of a story, and his tales are accordingly deficient in cohesion and compactness."[77]

Possibly because of pro-Irish and anti-British sentiments, possibly because of unprejudiced critical standards, Simms had a higher regard for contemporary Irish romancers than for their British fellows. He praises William Carleton mildly for his warmth and color, and his good sketches of Irish life, but objects to his lack of taste. He is more enthusiastic about Samuel Lover, "a rare good fellow," who strains too much after merriment at times but succeeds in depicting Irishmen who are true to life, and about Charles Lever, badly underrated by the English but nevertheless the author of novels that were well-constructed and alive with action.[78]

By contrast, the English G. P. R. James had turned himself into a highly popular romancer "by merely imitative

industry . . . through the paths opened by Walter Scott."[79]
In fact, Simms enjoyed James' works and freely proclaimed
that they had certain virtues, especially a "sustained and
lively interest,"[80] although it is exceedingly doubtful that he
approved of J. H. Hammond's comment that James knew
how to "throw in the words that bring the tear. . . . It is about
the *whole* of his secret of success, such as it is. He beats
Scott, Bulwer, Cooper and all of you here."[81] Simms was
not quite prepared to admit this, but he evidently counted
James not only as a worthy rival but also (at some time after
1852, when James was appointed British Consul at Norfolk)
as a personal friend: a notice in 1858 in the Charleston
Mercury was not "designed as a criticism," but only that
"I keep you in grateful recollection."[82] Simms as critic
knew full well that James was at a far remove from Scott;
Simms as reader and as friend liked James and his works.

For W. H. Ainsworth, and the other lesser English
writers of romance, he had only mild and qualified praise.
They drew for their material upon Eugene Sue, but they
did not "possess a tithe of his genius, his power, the skill with
which he combines, or the courage with which he conceives."
The English writers are nearer to Dumas, and possibly have
patterned their works after his, but the French romancer is
infinitely the superior in invention, in good taste, in variety
of costume and character, and in "the light and shade which
are essential to the picture."[83]

Sue and Dumas were unjustly neglected; so, for that
matter, were most novelists who wrote in any tongue other
than English. He thought that "Goethe was emphatically
the great artist of the age," and that his *Wilhelm Meister's
Apprenticeship* was second only to his *Faust;* it was in
fiction "the masterwork of the great author of Germany."
Simms objected heartily to the tendency to call Goethe's
Wilhelm Meister merely a domestic story; it was a fiction
designed for amusement, but it was at the same time "social,
political, and philosophical." In it, Goethe demonstrated
that through a "domestic story" an author could design a
book for profound thought and meditation.[84] To Simms,
this was undoubtedly the highest praise to be given to a
domestic novel, but when some reviewer thought an Italian
novel "the best specimen extant of Italian prose fiction," he

did not hesitate to pronounce it inferior to Manzoni's *I Promessi Sposi*.[85] Simms preferred in English or in Italian a book that showed or at least indicated originality. Few writers did that. Manzoni did.

So did the Brontës. Simms was at first convinced that the authors were men. In various notices he praised their hard masculinity and rough native powers, and was quite surprised in 1850 to read that the author of *Jane Eyre* (his favorite among the Brontë novels) was a woman. *Wuthering Heights* seemed "clumsy," but in Jane the heroine and the woman were fused, and the novel, in spite of some coldness, monotony, and lapses of taste, exhibited "design, as well in the persons as the story."[86] He found George Borrow harder to place, and doubted that he was a novelist at all, but anyone who would read *Lavengro* "with regard to the writer himself, as his own subject," would find it "eminently provocative and commonly interesting."[87]

His enthusiasm for Anthony Trollope was genuine but somewhat limited. Books like *Dr. Thorne* and *The Bertrams* were "charming works of fiction"; the author was "generally amiable and clever"; his works were not dull or tedious, but the highest praise that Simms could give them was that they "might be held truthful" and show an "extreme fidelity to nature."[88]

In the "Literary Docket," George Eliot was "charged with a volume of domestic fiction called Adam Bede." The critical jury pronounced it "a good moral story; Adam was declared to be an admirable fellow, and to have worked out his mission in society with credit to himself and family; and George Eliot, to whom we owe the creation of this Adam, was bade go and make as many more of the same sort of persons as he pleased." Unfortunately, in her next attempt, George Eliot did not fully succeed: *The Mill on the Floss* was not up to the earlier novel, although the "author of Adam Bede is incapable of a positively bad book—incapable of a book which shall not interest, and in which there shall not be picturesque development and fine characterization . . . the catastrophe seems in conflict with all our ideas, not only of poetical and human justice, but of completeness and propriety." George Eliot had been guilty of resorting to the device of the inferior playwrights, "according to Latin satire," in requiring a *deus ex machina* (the flood) to resolve the novel.

When he reviewed *Felix Holt*, Simms had to make even sharper reservations and distinctions. The reviewers "all conspired to praise her, even in the face of her evident deterioration as a *novelist*, as a teller of interesting and absorbing stories. We make this distinction carefully, for as a woman of genius, a master of strong, graphic, good English, a keen appreciation and delineation of scenery and character, she still holds the high position which she reached almost at a bound. . . . But who can as a story compare 'Felix Holt' with its long side issues of local political discussion, its impossible plots and improbable personages, with 'Adam Bede,' 'The mill on the Floss,' and the 'Scenes from Clerical Life.' "[89]

Although he was prejudiced against the English, he was not prejudiced against English novelists. Apparently he started a book with the idea, or at least the hope, that he would like it. It did not matter whether it was a romance, a novel, or a slightly fictionalized autobiography; if Simms could after reading the book picture himself like Borrow as "blackguard and breechless," it was for him a success. He read many books unemotionally, for the sake of the information they contained, but his first and his ultimate test of a novel was that it should move him emotionally and interest him intellectually. Scott could almost always do it; Dickens, most of the time; Thackeray, rarely. He told his readers bluntly his own reactions to a particular book. Whether or not these reactions were right or wise, they were entirely his own.

III

Quite possibly the best of Simms' critical essays is on James Fenimore Cooper. Bryant praised it highly; so did Trent. Certainly it deserves praise. Simms expresses many times his personal disgust at being called a follower or imitator of Cooper, but Cooper was the best of American novelists; Cooper as writer had many defects, but his positive virtues had never been fully acknowledged; Simms attempted (and in the main succeeded) to point out the bad and the preponderantly good in Cooper's work. It is a magnanimous essay, yet even today it seems just.

Cooper's most notable achievement in *The Spy* and later

romances was to open "the eyes of our people to their own resources." It was Cooper who "first awakened" Americans and Englishmen to a new and indigenous literature. Washington Irving with his "sweet and delicate essays" had not done this, for he "was not accounted in England an American writer, and he . . . took no pains to assert his paternity." Cooper let it be clearly understood that he was an American writer, and in his conflicts between hunters and Indians, in pursuits, flights, traps, pitfalls, captures and rescues, in cunning opposed to cunning, "Mr. Cooper has no superior as he has had no master." True, his conception of the frontiersman was "less true than picturesque," and even the redoubtable Hawkeye was a "sailor in a hunting shirt," but the intensity that marked Cooper's best work made these portrayals "as perfect, of their kind, as the artist of fiction has ever given us."[90]

Cooper depended too much on highly dramatic scenes, and too little on a carefully-wrought design. The defect in *The Spy*, Simms thought, "was rather in its action than in its characters. This is the usual and grand defect in all Mr. Cooper's stories." But the author more than compensated for these defects by "felicitous display of scenery," by "fine moral and dramatic pictures," by "intensifying every subject which affects his mind," and above all by superb native characters acting out their dramas in a native scene.[91] Simms had no patience with local critics who carpingly denigrated Cooper's achievement by emphasizing his defects and minimizing his positive accomplishments, and he protested vigorously against such treatment of the first writer "to begin fairly the career of American letters."[92]

From his earliest days as a magazine editor, Simms had ardently encouraged the development of a national and a regional literature. When in 1828 he and James Wright Simmons started the *Southern Literary Gazette*, they announced in the Prospectus that their primary object was "to encourage the efforts and do justice to the claims of native genius. . . . The Editors invite the contributions of the literary gentlemen in general, and especially of the South. Favors from their own immediate townsmen will not, they trust, be withheld." These sentences might have fittingly served as an introductory to most of the magazines that

Simms later edited. Consistent also with his later point of view was the insistence that our literature must be emancipated "from its present state of feudal bondage and allegiance to those 'Master Spirits' of Great Britain."[93]

Simms (perhaps with the collaboration of his fellow-editors) re-stated his belief in native genius in "Le Debut," the prefatory article in *The Cosmopolitan* (1833). There was abundant talent in country, state, and city, but too often it found an outlet only in turbulent partisan controversy.[94] Although they did not invite outside contributions, the authors hoped that as pioneers they would encourage their fellow-citizens to write.

For those men who wrote even reasonably good American books, there should be just recognition, and their Americanism should be noted as a virtue. When he asked permission to dedicate *The Damsel of Darien* to James Kirke Paulding, he put it on the ground that Paulding was "among the most successful of our native authors,—as indeed, one of the fathers of our forest literature,—a leading Pioneer,"[95] and in the Preface itself as an author who had "never made any concessions to . . . foreign sway."[96] He did not care greatly for Paulding as a humorist, thinking him successful only in "his least ambitious efforts,"[97] but "admired him more as a downright sensible writer, hearty, frank and unaffected"; his work was not highly spiced, but it was not likely to pall upon the appetite.

Although he was on friendly terms with Robert Montgomery Bird and John Pendleton Kennedy, exchanged new books with them, and dedicated a book to each one, he was never unrestrainedly enthusiastic about their work. Bird's *Adventures of Robin Day* and, surprisingly, Kennedy's *Rob of the Bowl* he described as "very small performances."[98] Bird's work was "rich in merit," but except in *Nick of the Woods* he tended to dissipate his fictional energies on too many characters and to give too much information that, though "highly useful," is "out of place in such a rapid work as the romance";[99] Kennedy, "one of our most accomplished authors and orators,"[100] was better: in *Swallow Barn* he had given "genial and natural pictures of Virginia Life" and had effectively answered the abolitionists.[101] *Horse-Shoe Robinson* was even better, but here Kennedy had trespassed on Simms' own territory, and Simms in a letter warned him that "I join issue with you upon certain points of your Historical Summary, and suggest some shortcomings in the details of the story. . . . But all my fault-finding is done lovingly I think, and will not ruffle your plumage."[102]

He noticed the book first in an omnibus review, "Domestic Histories of the South," and then in an article-review. In each he wrote that Kennedy is "one of our favorites"; and *Horse-Shoe Robinson* is "one of our most stirring and truthful native fictions,"[103] and an "admirable characteristic narrative."[104] In dedicating *Count Julian* to Kennedy, Simms regretted that it was unworthy, but might serve as "one of the best of my own abilities, and of my respect for yours."

For Edgar Allan Poe as man and as critic Simms had mixed feelings and many reservations. Poe had brought many of his difficulties upon himself. "He is undoubtedly a man of very peculiar and very considerable genius—but is irregular and exceedingly mercurial in his temperament."[105] He was given to feuding and mystifying; he needed, Simms advised him, to "cast away those pleasures which are not worthy of your mind, and to trample those temptations underfoot, which degrade your person.[106] Moreover, as critic Poe had first noticed Simms by a "very savage attack on one of my novels"—*The Partisan*. The critical remarks on the story and the style might have been justified, although portions of the review were not just. But Poe had unfairly made his comments "rude and offensive and personal." These were grave defects, and Simms was not inclined to forget or to minimize them.[107]

Nevertheless, for Poe as creative writer he had the highest respect. After listing his grievances to Evert A. Duyckinck, Simms wrote that "He has more real imaginative power than 99 in the 100 of our poets and tale writers. His style is clear and correct, his conceptions bold and fanciful, his fancies vivid, and his taste generally good. His bolder effects are impaired by his fondness for *detail* and this hurts his criticism which is too frequently given to the analysis of the inferior points of style, making him somewhat regardless of the more noble features of the work. But, I repeat, he is a man of remarkable power."[108] In 1845 he added significantly to this estimate: Poe in his stories is "a writer of rare imaginative excellence, great intensity of mood, and a singularly mathematical directness of purpose . . . nothing more original, of their kind, has ever been given to the American reader."[109] The following year, in reviewing Poe's poetry, Simms added a larger note of praise by saying that "Some of his stories are the most remarkable specimens of the power of *intensifying* a conception of pure romance, to the exclusion of all the ordinary agents of fiction, which have been written."[110]

In his own imaginative stories Simms admitted a resemblance to those of Poe, "and partially of Hawthorne."[111] At times the latter was a "delicate, essayical prose writer," but he frequently wrote with the intensity of a poet, and he was always "quite unaffected" in his genius. Although a "tale writer, rather than a novelist . . . he has a rare and delicate fancy"; and though his range was limited, he was truthful in his delineation of character. Simms compared Hawthorne's "distribution" of light and shade with that of the ablest Italian painters, while his mind penetrated to the origin and the substance of evils. *The Scarlet Letter* had tremendous "concentrative power," but *The House of the Seven Gables* was "more truthful" to life. His domain in fiction was "peculiarly this fine one of the heart," and he entered, "with the art of Sterne, into the heart of his single captive." He was a "minute philosopher" and psychologist who lacked interest in action. *The Blithedale Romance* seemed "quite as successful" as the earlier novels: "It has all their defects, and these defects are such as seem inseparable from the author's mind. These lie chiefly in the shaping and conception of the work and in the inadequate employment of his characters."[112] Yet these were but minor blemishes, and Simms acknowledged that he had learned much from Hawthorne.

When he reviewed *The Marble Faun*, Simms not only praised the novel highly as showing "no falling off of his high powers"; he also wrote a rounded and glowing tribute to Hawthorne as author: "He is a man of genius, a man of fine original conceptions; of a taste at once delicate and masculine; of a nice blending of the sanguine and the spiritual; of exquisite sentiment; and a just recognition, along with it, of the sensuous and human. He cannot write commonplaces; and his readers, even when he may happen to fail utterly, as he rarely does, of the object at which he aims, will always, in spite of all failures, feel themselves in the keeping of one who not only thinks for himself, but will require them to do some thinking also. His genius is not of the bold and passionate order; he does not deal with men in masses, or with men in progress; hardly with men in action. In other words, he has few dramatic characteristics. But he has certain dramatic elements. He has design; he has fancy; can conceive, and enter into deep devotional moods. . . . He has the characteristic of the novelist; blending sentiment and a modified form of passion with reverie and contemplation."[113]

His opinion of Herman Melville was less clear-cut. Soon after 1840 Simms loosely allied himself with Evert Duyckinck, Cornelius Mathews, and the "Young America" movement. The members of this group or movement were almost violently advocating a distinctive American literature. Melvile was Duyckinck's protégé, and Simms was genuinely fond of Duyckinck. Moreover, "Young America" was the sworn enemy of Lewis Gaylord Clark and the conservative critics, and in this period, as Perry Miller has phrased it, "the *Knickerbocker's* notices of Simms were concentrated poison, and those in the *Mirror* downright nasty."[114] Simms felt close enough to the group to write Duyckinck in 1844 that his projected *Southern and Western Magazine* would "in some measure afford us the organ we desire. Until you can get your press in N. Y. you must be content with a wing of it in Charleston."[115]

In adddition, Simms apparently liked Melville and remembered him with some affection, for as late as 1867 he wrote that if he had known that Melville's brother was in Charleston, he would in spite of illness have called on Allan Melville.[116] As early as April of 1846 Simms had reviewed *Typee* enthusiastically, though he treated it as a travel book rather than as a novel: "a very curious and interesting narrative of savage life, and well deserving perusal . . . . We have every reason to believe that Mr. Melville is a veracious chronicler though it must be confessed he tells a very strange and romantic story."[117] *White Jacket* was convincing enough in its exposé of abuses in the Navy that it deserved "the equal consideration of government and people,"[118] and *Red-*

burn had much to commend it to the reader. But Simms thought *Mardi* a much better book; "wild, improbable and fantastic as was that allegorical production," it yet gave more proof of "real powers in reserve" than Melville's other work.[119] This was no slight concession on Simms' part, for Melville had done his best to spoil the work for Southern readers by painting "a loathsome picture of Mr. Calhoun, in the character of a slave driver drawing mixed blood and tears from the victim at every stroke of the whip."[120]

It is surprising that Simms liked the book at all, for this "fanciful voyage about the world in search of happiness" violated completely his tenet that prose fiction should be founded upon "common sense" in handling of characters and incidents as well as in philosophy. But even this qualified approval disappeared utterly when he reviewed *Moby Dick*. Although the sections on whales and whaling were "very interesting," the book itself was "sad stuff and dreary or ridiculous." In fact, the "ravings" of Captain Ahab and "those of Mr. Melville are such as would justify a *writ de lunatico* against all parties."[121] *Pierre* baffled him completely, and he confessed to his readers that he greatly feared Melville should be "put in ward," for he has gone "clean daft . . . certainly he has given us a very mad book, my masters."[122]

When he disapproved of a book, Simms had little regard for the reputation of the author. An anonymous novel, *The Swamp Steed*, revealed the writer's complete ignorance of South Carolina, as to terrain, people, and dialect. This was a defect of knowledge as well as of art.[123] Longfellow's *Kavanagh* failed for an entirely different reason: in spite of some passages of "beauty and felicity," it had only a "slight and commonplace" moral.[124] By 1845 Simms was also likely to be aroused to wrath by attacks on the South, and to damn a book for that reason alone: even his friend Catherine Maria Sedgwick, "one of our favorites—one of those writers whom we always find it very safe to commend" was castigated (in Simms' own words, "I shall be constrained to reproach her gently") for her "unnecessary flings at the South."[125]

A puzzling yet amusing example of his surprisingly rare surrender to sectional prejudice came much later. In 1859 he wrote a mediumly favorable review of John W. De

Forest's *Seacliff*, although it was weak in invention, "except in the *dénouement*." He implies also that he knew De Forest personally. When in 1867 he reviewed *Miss Ravenel's Conversion from Secession to Loyalty*, the infuriated Simms declared (forgetting, or deliberately disclaiming, any previous knowledge) that it was by a writer who "seems to have done other works, of which we know nothing." The novel is "the embodiment of all the brutal malignity Northern writers have ever conceived, or reported, to the slander and misrepresentation of the South." As De Forest lacked "the art-faculty of Mrs. Stowe," the book had in it nothing remarkable except its "intense malignity, which has blackened every page with a slander, and pointed every paragraph with a lie."[126]

Since he did not like Cornelius Mathews or his writings but heartily approved his fight for an international copyright and for an original American literature, Simms asked Evert Duyckinck to review *Big Abel and the Little Manhattan* (1845) for his *Southern and Western Magazine*.[127] He published what seemed to him an excessively laudatory review, for the novel was "too entirely New York" to interest those readers who were not familiar with the city: "A more qualified language in his behalf, would not only be more just, but much more kind." When the *Knickerbocker* attacked Mathews, Duyckinck counterattacked. Simms thought that Lewis Clark deserved to be "scourged hip and thigh. . . . But you have erred in making his assault upon Mathews your particular text. . . . He is confessedly your *questio vexata* in New York. Wilful in the employment of his talents, rejecting wholesome counsel and quarreling with those who bestow it, he perversely wars not less upon his own genius than upon public opinion." Simms recognized Mathews as an ambitious and sometimes an able writer, but his mind was essentially undramatic: "He seems fettered and frigid when his business is to develop his story through the medium of other agents. He does not succeed in grouping, and seems to lack the required flexibility—the capacity to enter into the characters of his persons, and to speak only in obedience to their necessities."[128]

Toward the younger Southern novelists Simms assumed the role of a generous but just mentor, who did not hesitate to tender advice both privately and publicly. This can be illustrated by two letters to John Esten Cooke, and two notices of his work. In July 1859 he advised the younger author to "work freely and frequently in papers which do not involve invention. Your error has been to have striven to write in fiction with as little reserve as in narrative and facts—topics. This cannot be done with safety. Fiction requires invention, more elaborate design, your whole heart as well as head; and these demand frequent pauses, when the Imagination may repose, and, looking up, catch new inspirations." Cooke scattered his energy and "divided the reader's attention among too many personages"; he was chiefly successful in "the liveliness and piquancy of the dialogue, and the saliency of feature in some of your portraits."[129]

Strictures and praise were repeated in an article that is mainly a tribute to the entire family, "John Esten Cooke of Virginia," in the Charleston *Mercury*, October 21, 1859, although Simms added the consolatory judgment that Cooke "is now one of the most eminent of novel writers in the country."

When *Henry St. John, Gentleman* was published later that same year, Simms warned Cooke that "I find fault, as matter of course."[130] There is in Simms' notice in the *Mercury* a reasonable amount of praise for Cooke's portrayal of Virginia, for his doing justice to his section, and for his "life-like portraits"; there is qualified praise for the story as "lively, well sustained and interesting, without being deeply tragical, or intensively acting upon the imaginative and nervous systems"; there is also severe admonishment to the author: "He has done well, so far; but his sinews must be a little more seasoned by the proper exercise; his mind more patient, more deliberate, more sensible of the burden of the task, more grandly stirred within him, by the hourly growing sense of the value of his theme, so that he shall shape it with proper care, with a becoming purpose, and under a severer, sublimer design."[131] However unwelcome, this was excellent advice, though it must have seemed ironical to Cooke that it should come from William Gilmore Simms.

In his post-war reviews, Simms welcomed new or unfamiliar novelists, although he continued to distribute praise and fault-finding in what seemed to him a judicious manner. Two examples will suffice. He thought that *Dallas Galbreath*, by Rebecca Harding Davis, was a "strange compound of a good story well told, with characters that do violence to the popular conception of nature. . . . in the conception of the plot she has displayed considerable tact and skill, and in her portrayings of the characters she has met in one or two instances with success."[132] More interesting is his treatment of Sidney Lanier's *Tiger-Lilies*. Since he was familiar with some of the author's "quaint, vigorous little poems," Simms expected to find the novel "sketchy, disconnected, strong, nervous, rhythmical—and we have not, on the whole, been disappointed." It was almost plotless, with little dialogue; but it was eminently suggestive, with a wealth of "illustration and poetic analogy." Sectional pride was still strong in Simms: "Southern literature may well thank Mr. Lanier for giving it a child of which it need not feel ashamed."[133]

IV

Simms' reviews, like his letters, were written hastily, with little or no revision. He intended to present fairly the intention of the author, as well as to judge his achievement, for he firmly believed that the "standards of good criticism require that the reader should glow with the same element which inspires the writer."[134] And he had thought long if not very systematically about literature. Like most nineteenth-century critics, he had discarded the idea that the universe is a harmonious machine for the concept that it is a growing organism. Likewise the literary work should grow under the hand of the novelist, but it should develop organically into a planned design.[135]

In a somewhat elaborate comparison, Simms depicts the growth of the novel as resembling the progress of a traveler taking a day's walk. He has companions; he passes through a varied landscape in variable weather; he is sometimes beguiled from the path; but toward the close of day he arrives at the object of his quest.[136] Yet all must be harmonious, in a way that actual life or history rarely shows it to be: "Hence, it is the artist only who is the true historian. It

is he who gives shape to the unknown fact,—who yields
relation to the scattered fragments,—who unites the parts in
coherent dependency, and endows, with life and action, the
otherwise motionless automata of history."[137]

Simms rarely achieved this goal in his own fiction; he
was often fallible in judging the achievements of others.
But he was constantly aware that such a goal existed. However imperfectly shaped and used, it gave a consistent and
reasonably philosophical basis for his criticism.

CHAPTER III

On Poetry and Poets

"I REGARD Poetry as the profoundest of human philosophies," wrote Simms in 1854; "poetry is the mysterious voice of the deeper nature lying in the heart, or in the depths of the great Nature spreading about and above us."[1] Poetry seemed to him "the foundation of the fine arts,"[2] and the finest expression of man's thought, his imagination, and his fancy. Many people thought of it as merely "a soothing pastime for writer and reader," and demanded little more of it than "lucid and liquid commonplaces."[3] This was a vulgar error. There might well be legitimate disagreements about the definition of poetry or the merits of a poet, but "his humanity, like his genius" must be catholic. Any writer worthy of the name drew his inspiration from the "deepest fountains of philosophy. He is not your versifier, simply. He is a thinker, a seeker, a discoverer, a creator."[4]

Poetry is "thought delivered in music . . . born of beauty";[5] it is "among the best agencies," and in some respects superior to formal religion, "to procure for us that wing which alone can lift us above the world." This did not imply vagueness, except insofar as it enabled the poet to escape from the literal: "Directness of aim, and concentration of thought do not necessarily imply the literal, and these, with Imagination and Fancy, as a decorative quality, are the whole source of power in poetry, and so of permanent reputation. Poetry is winged thought. It must be thought; this, founded upon close observation of man and nature, the moral and physical world. . . . Such, we find in Homer, Aeschylus, Milton, Dante, Shakspeare, and other great masters of the past. . . . To think and feel in poetry is the true secret."[6]

Simms had started writing poetry when he was about

eight years old; although the bulk of his verse was written before he was thirty, throughout his life he continued to write new poems and to re-write and to publish his youthful verses. His real forte, he sometimes claimed, was in writing poetry instead of prose, and he was troubled and angry at his lack of recognition in this field. He wrote E. A. Duyckinck that "I flatter myself that my poetical works exhibit the highest phase of the Imaginative faculty which this country has yet exhibited, and the most philosophical in connection with it."[7] Even his youthful friend and admirer Paul Hamilton Hayne found this a gross misjudgment; when Simms fancied himself as a throw-back to the rugged Elizabethans, Hayne shuddered privately, however much he was willing to praise and defend Simms publicly.[8]

If he over-valued his poetry, Simms was certain that the so-called practical men erroneously undervalued all poetry. To be known as a poet or painter was directly harmful to a lawyer or a businessman, but this was based on a false notion of what was useful. In various articles and in a long unpublished lecture, "Poetry and the Practical," Simms developed his idea that religion and philosophy must teach "the worship of the *Ideal* as a corrective against the dangers of the *Real*."[9] Both the English and the Americans were eminently practical, but they were too much concerned with external and material conquests, too little with spiritual values (2-4).

In a discussion of the Bible and of the moral laws of God, Simms presents man as serving a kind of apprenticeship on earth before reaching a state of true goodness after death (9-14). God presents himself to man not through the Church and the Bible only, but through Nature and Art (here, specifically, poetry) as well. In phrasings reminiscent of Wordsworth and Emerson, Simms praises the daily-recurring miracles of nature, and the ability of the uncorrupted child-heart to absorb its lessons (15-26). But men generally lack the ability to understand or to interpret. Here the poet must take over. Poetry has a minor use when it deals with man and the earth, with thoughts and moods, but at its best poetry helps us to turn from the animal and the inferior to the intellect and the divine (26-27; I, 15-18). For the poet is "the Prince of abstract ideas . . . the material is simply the medium for the expression of that imaginative truth which he possessed long before he gave to shape to it in song." Paraphrasing Michelangelo, he agreed that the sculptor "beholds the statue in the rock, long before he seeks to give it outline with his chisel" (29-30). Figuratively, the poet works in the same way. Through the "Divine form of language," the poet "indicates the possible *real* to which the future may attain." Thus the abstract of today becomes the practical of tomorrow: "it is the shadow of the approaching *Reality*" (37-38).

Poetry had usefulness for the future, but it had even greater value with regard to the past: "I regard fiction, so-called, as embodying the largest amount of truth in possession of the race . . . to him who properly comprehends the laws of fiction,—and who sees in the design of Poet and Romancer, nothing less than a constant struggle to grasp at the most general and invariable of the truths of nature—truths that survive, and are consequently superior in their integrity, to all the changes, customs, habits and fashions of mankind—truths which survive races" (43). Elaborating on this point, Simms asked if anyone now doubted "that Shakspeare was the most practically wise man of his day in Europe?" His plays are worth more than political or philosophical essays; they are "all profound lessons in philosophy" (II, 29).

Inspiration embodied in art strengthens the intellect, but it sustains the soul. Many people feel the need of church and priesthood for spiritual sustenance, but there are valuable and neglected auxiliaries in nature and art (47-67). For the poets were the first priests and prophets, and the "true Poet is one who brings us daily revelations of new truth, from him who is the source of all truth" (70-73). Poetry also is rich in its variety, and capable of appealing to all tastes and classess. For the unlettered, there was "Homer, singing from door to door. For the noble and the stately, the refined and lettered . . . ministrels like Tasso and Ariosto, like Virgil and Campbell. For young Hearts, there is the earnest, and amorous Burns, and the passionate Byron; for the universal heart there is Shakspeare; Homer lights the fires of war, illuminates the wastes of history, and persuades to Fame; Wordsworth beguiles the soberer mood to contemplation, and Milton and Dante wing the Soul for Heaven with all the ardors of a Divine Enthusiasm. Enthusiasm, in fact, is the high and holy gift which the Poet imparts to Society; and enthusiasm is the great antagonist quality opposed to Self;—the vital element which informs all the nobler passions" (74).

When he enlarged the essay, Simms added an introductory section on early English poets. He began with a tribute to Chaucer as "the Father of English verse—a statesman,—an Ambassador abroad, shrewd always and sensible,—yet a Poet, with a genius at once tender and masculine—with an art that could persuade the loveliest landscapes to his canvas, yet depict, in the foreground, the homeliest aspects, true to the life, of his own rugged people; a delightful humorist, a sharp satirist, a man of keen observation and calm, discriminating judgment." Although not masters, Wyatt and Surrey were worthy followers who "refined upon the language of Chaucer." In life and in poetry, Sidney was an exemplar of "refined chivalry." But Spenser was the "first great poet after Chaucer. . . . What a rich variety, in thought and language, grace and strength, marches on, like an army, with the pomp of banners, and the joy of music, in his quaint array" (I, 1-3).

These English poets, with Gower, shaped our language. Other poets in other lands had done the same, often (as with Schiller) at a material self-sacrifice, partly because they minister to "all the wants of our nature—not as the nature of an animal,—but as the nature of a God" (III, 3). The poets have shaped language, preserved history, informed philosophy, and inspired science. Simms believed in the richness of the inner life and in the reliability of intuition; he believed in the civilizing powers of the fine arts, and especially of poetry; he believed that in this sense poetry was practical.

The self-described utilitarians were bent only on quick and immediate gains. They were short-sighted. Even of authors they demanded only something equivalent to the tyranny of trade, a rapid success commensurate to the hours of employment. In Simms' estimation, these values were false, and therefore ultimately non-utilitarian: "as the Literature of every nation constitutes its most enduring and honorable monuments, it follows that permanence and premeditation must enter largely into the spirit with which

the laborer sits down to his task. The works of genius are
labors always; not sports."[10] Now and then, a well-trained
man might by accident achieve greatness through a casual
production, but this seemed to him unlikely.

At the same time, he preferred to trust, for shorter lyrics,
to impulse rather than to art. When Hayne objected to
the lack of artistry in some of his works, Simms objected
vigorously if not quite coherently: the lyrics "are *not* fugi-
tives at all. They are mostly remarkable *improvisations*, refined
subsequently by exquisite art—*Happy Inspiration. I object
to studies of art* in a province which implies improvisation
—lyrics really being bird gushes—involuntaries—unpremeditated."[11] In another letter he speaks of his lyrics as being
"overflowings," and suggests that his correspondents do
not understand the nature of the lyric. It may be that Hayne
was more nearly right when he wrote that Simms was reluctant
to undertake the onerous task of correction and revision.[12]

Yet there seems no reason to believe that Simms was not
here expressing an honest opinion. W. P. Trent states dogmatically that Simms not only did not know how to write a
sonnet, but did not have much idea of what a sonnet should
be.[13] Unfortunately Trent mentions but does not reckon
with Simms' trenchant if highly prejudiced remarks about
English and Italian sonnets. Sensuous love sonnets could be
written in the sinuous and flexible Italian language. But in
English the strict form was a fetter, and "its uses will com-
port only with such grave subjects as demand severity,
enjoin dignity and exhibit power and thought, and moral
and will." In reviewing Hayne's *Avolio* (1860) Simms warns
his friend that the love sonnets of Wyatt and Surrey are
forgotten; Sidney and Milton chose the form not because
of its appropriateness but because they were passionately
fond of Italian letters; Shakspeare was wise enough to blend
the metaphysical with the sensuous, yet his sonnets are
"unlike and inferior in music, to the wonderful musical
effects and exquisite felicities of his blank verse!" Of all
the English writers Wordsworth has "in his political and
ecclesiastical sonnets, done best of all . . . but, even in his
hands, as in those of Milton, we still doubt if anything has
been gained, by the thought, in the rigid form chosen for
its utterance." [14]

Simms was not exactly ignorant of Italian literature; his translation of Dante's "Paolo and Francesca" episode was called by Theodore Koch in his *Dante in America* highly creditable, and Simms was familiar with Italian poetry and novels. But he did not agree with Leigh Hunt and with Hayne [15] that the Italian or "legitimate" sonnet was superior to the English, "a thing of freedom." The best of English sonnets, he thought, belonged to what was "somewhat improperly styled the *Illegitimate* Sonnet." As far as Simms was concerned, there were only two rules: a single leading idea (in this he was a bit more rigorous than Longfellow or Frost) and compression into fourteen lines.

The flexible Tuscan language lent itself to an exact art form and to the language of love; the sterner and less flexible English did not regard "with much esteem the dexterity which delights to multiply its fetters"; in the sonnet, as in all his other works, he did not set much value on "pure art." Rather, he valued moral differences: the Italians were "given mostly to themes of tenderness, love and fanciful sentiment. But English and American Poets cannot make love in Sonnets. The very severity and rigidity of the rule of art in the Sonnet is unfavorable to the expression of an earnest passion." Even Shakspeare's sonnets when they deal only with love indicate how seriously they are "infected by this weakness." But English and American poets had used the sonnet for "sterner purposes." As it had developed in these countries, Simms believed, the sonnet was a "bolder, braver, manlier thing than the Italian, and you cannot in all the collections of Italy find any Sonnets to compare in thought, grandeur, dignity, a sonorous emphasis, or masculine majesty" with those of Shakspeare, Milton, or Wordsworth. He also won George H. Boker's gratitude by calling him the best of American sonnet writers and the "most really able, various and powerful of all the poets which the Northern States have produced."[16]

He was more interested in content than in form. He was divided in writing poetry, he wrote R. W. Griswold, "between the desire to appear correct, and the greater desire to be original and true."[17] He set little store on certain of the grace notes of poetry. Rhyme seemed to him "the mere decoration of thought,"[18] and verse was essentially that, also.

In a letter to James Lawson, Simms defended his prose romance *The Damsel of Darien* on the ground that it "is, indeed, a Poem."[19] His words in The Prefatory Letter to *The Yemassee* are more moderate: the romance is the "substitute which the people of the present day offer for the ancient epic. . . . It approximates the poem." But neither verse nor rhyme seemed to him essential in poetry. Unavailingly and perhaps a bit obtusely he advised Thomas Holley Chivers to "seek for simplicity and wholeness. . . . Be manly, direct, simple, natural—be full, unaffected and elaborate."[20] This described what Simms sought for in both the reading and writing of poetry.

He coveted fame as a writer and recognized that it could best be gained through imaginative works: "A fine song or a sonnet will make a reputation when a grave history will be forgotten. . . . Contemporaries seldom see this. They are more impressed with shows of labor and research than of invention. Were Shakspeare and Sir Thomas More now living, the latter would take rank of the former amongst all contemporaries. Yet look at the past! It is through the poets of the Hebrew; Homer and Aeschylus of the Greeks; Horace and Virgil among the Romans; Milton, Chaucer, Spenser, Shakspeare, among the English; Lope de Vega and Calderon among the Spaniards, etc., all writers of the imagination—poets simply," that later generations know and understand even the "histories of their several countries."[21] Hoping to be remembered, even if not in such august company, Simms published his poems (frequently at his own expense) in order to "put myself on record" for posterity.[22]

II

In his early poetry Simms was most powerfully and directly influenced by Byron; in his later, by Wordsworth, "the greatest of all the tribe of contemplative poets. From 15 to 40 a man of blood enjoys Byron and Moore. After that he asks for the food of thought, and not of passion."[23] He did not consider them the greatest of English poets. Definitely ahead of them were Shakspeare, with his "universal song. . . . The mighty master-hand in his we trace"; Chaucer, who with his "healthy Muse" won respect for "native England's *tongue*"; probably Spenser, artful and mystifying, with his ability to "spiritualize the passionate, and subdue/ The wild, coarse temper of the British Muse"; and certainly Milton, a "Prophet Bard" with a "godlike voice" that allied earth to heaven.[24]

These were the giants. Even Wordsworth, with his "voice of purest thought in sweetest music,"[25] came behind them. As Simms uses the term, *contemplative* is by no means an unmixed compliment, for the "contemplative writer is usually a phlegmatic in temperament," who does not arouse the emotions as do writers like Scott and Byron who "appeal to the blood and the brain in common."[26] Wordsworth is neither a philosopher nor a philosophical poet; he is "certainly a thoughtful poet, but his reflections are not the results of laborious reasoning, but the suggestions of a meditative genius." He had no "predecessor of equal genius" in descriptive poetry. His pictures of natural scenery were at once felicitous and faithful, but through associations and analogies he allied the moral with the physical, the internal with the external. Except in the Lucy poems, there is little passion, and there is no sense of epic or dramatic action, but there are compensations: *The Excursion* has in it "more exquisite simplicity and purity of style than any approaching the same length since *Paradise Lost* was written," and *The Prelude* is "full of passages marked by his earnest sweetness, the grave delicacy of his mood, his habit of musing contemplation, and the rare philosophical simplicity which makes the analysis of his mind and writings so interesting."[27]

The Prelude seemed to him Wordsworth's finest poem. It is essentially the "biography of Wordsworth. There he has told us all it is necessary to know. . . . His great poem is the history of his own mind." Scott and Byron could be imitated because "they were more of artists," but although many had tried, no one had successfully imitated Wordsworth, for while never neglecting art, he had an individual philosophy of life: "An art may to some extent be acquired or borrowed, its tricks be learnt, but great principles must beget their own facts."[28] As a poet, Wordsworth had certain limitations that Simms recognized and pointed out, but he also thought Wordsworth easily the greatest of modern poets writing in English. It would be many years before a successor embodied in his work so many excellent qualities.[29]

Wordsworth had "done more than any other man to direct the tendencies and form the school of modern poetry," but he had been wrongly credited with being "the chief author of the cleansing process to which our English poetry had been subjected. To Cowper belongs this credit in the highest degree." It was William Cowper, not Wordsworth, who had rescued our poetry from "the sway of French taste and authority in letters," and he protested that both English and American critics had consistently underrated Cowper's achievement. For Cowper was a moral poet, of "admirable fancy, humor and wit," and of strong though not discursive imaginative faculties springing from a "singularly independent" mind.[30]

Simms was not belittling the value of Wordsworth's poetry or his poetic theories, but simply giving credit to an improperly neglected writer. He never doubted that Wordsworth was greater than Cowper, just as he was greater than Coleridge, who "had, perhaps, a richer and more inventive mind, a larger range of knowledge, quicker affections, and a more fiery enthusiasm. But he has left behind him no great monument to assert his unquestionable genius."[31] For Robert Southey he had at that time less regard, for in grace and beauty his poetry was inferior to Coleridge's, as in sustained and elevated poetic thought it was inferior to Wordsworth's. Much later, he praised Southey as a man, in spite of his partisanship, and wrote that "the grand and grotesque conceptions of his muse have never found a just, capable, and appreciative critic."[32]

In Byron's work Simms was conscious of passion and power. Certain parts of *Childe Harold* seemed to him "noble verses . . . they stir my blood as the sound of a trumpet. The feeling of which they speak, is not only elevated, but what is more, it is natural and true."[33] But for all his attractiveness, there was in Byron and in his poetry a considerable flaw: if he had not given way to self-pity and licentiousness, "His muse had been triumphant over Time/ As still she is o'er Passion."[34] In the Preface to *Donna Florida*, Simms hoped that he "might imitate the grace and exceeding felicity of expression in that unhappy performance (*Don Juan*)—its playfulness, and possibly its wit—without falling into its licentiousness of utterance and malignity of mood." Yet he felt, characteristically, that he had gone beyond imitation and achieved something original.[35]

Byron's aspirations had been greater than his performances. He was discontented with what he had done; if he had lived, he might have written far greater poems, since his "was not the vain, small spirit to be satisfied with the successes he had won."[36] Although Simms once called *Don Juan* "that book of excellently expressed commonplaces,"[37] he believed that Byron had revealed one phase of romanticism better than any other poet: his "Harold, his Manfred, nay, even his Don Juan, are full of strains whose true import is that of the stricken soul—the haunted conscience—the heart yearning for repose, and beginning to despair of hope."[38] He was a poet "of the terrific and intenser passions," but where Dante or Milton could give a scene "in a few bold touches . . . Byron has given it in details."[39]

Sir Walter Scott had none of the personal defects of Byron. As a writer of romances he stood supreme; as poet, he was like Homer in the rush and sweep of his action but he had achieved only a limited "trumpet lay of chivalry and pride."[40] This was a restricted but not a negligible achievement in *The Lady of the Lake* and other verse romances "such as Scott has rendered so familiar to us, in that happy combination of the epic and the ballad which is destined to a long association with his peculiar genius." There could be found a model that American poets could use advantageously in treating such native legends as that of Pocahontas.[41]

Like Byron and unlike Scott, Robert Burns had noticeable personal defects. To Simms he was a man "of pride and sorrows, weak yet strong/ With still a song discoursing to the heart." He was a "melancholy conqueror," a man of "capricious genius" who held mastery over his art but not over his "own irregular soul."[42] Simms used Burns to advantage through his alter-ego, the partisan-poet George Dennison, who like Burns was a writer of native melodies, rude perhaps but "sweet and simple, and withal very touching."[43] Burns had also a secondary strength: because of his desire to "make some song which would live

'for poor old Scotland's sake,' " many of his songs possessed
for his readers "a sort of symbolical influence," and Burns
gained added power because he spoke "in the fulness of
his own soul, and from the overflowings of a burdened
heart." This was an incidental value that accrued to the
national poet, for his song was that of "an aroused and
earnest mind," and this impassioned earnestness roused like
emotions in his readers. [44]

Although in casual, unchecked quotations he sometimes
confused lines by Shelley and Keats,[45] Simms after the war
desired to replace his destroyed copies of their works,[46] and
he included Shelley in a poem on a group of poets, charac-
terizing him as "a changeling" who sang "Vague min-
strelsies," but whose "spiritual" voice leavened the earthi-
ness of the times.[47] By 1828 he was familiar with their work;
in an otherwise damning review in the *Southern Literary
Gazette* of Leigh Hunt's *Lord Byron and his Contemporaries*, the anonymous reviewer digresses to note that the
"only portion of the book worth reading, is the account of
Shelley and Keats—men of genius both, the latter of high
promise, and untimely end." Shelley's personal frailties had
not only brought him personal misery but ended his hopes
of "high distinction as a poet." He thought better of Keats,
who "had published very little, but that little is we think of
a high order."[48] The next year Simms, this time clearly in
his own right, praised Keats as "possessed of a high degree
of promise" and stated that "In some future notice, we
shall speak of him more at large."[49] If this notice was ever
written, it has not been identified.

Alfred Tennyson seemed a worthy successor to Wordsworth, although inferior to the older poet. Tennyson
deserved praise, for he "has the spirituality of Shelley,
without his intensity, and the contemplative nature of Wordsworth, with much more enthusiasm." Except for *In Memo-
riam*, which tended to become monotonous, he combined
artistry, subtlety, and variety.[50] But Tennyson's great popularity and the ease with which he could be imitated presented a great danger to young poets: Simms advised Charles
Warren Stoddard that "You must study Tennyson less,
and the earlier masters more. You should get back to Milton,
Shakspeare, and Dryden."[51]

As early as July, 1848, Simms knew Robert Browning's work and admired it enough to include a stanza on him for a book of poems on poets, edited by Caroline Gilman. Although Mrs. Gilman used only the section on Scott, Simms had included verses on most of the English poets that he liked: Chaucer, Spenser, Milton, Shakspeare. Byron, Scott, Burns, Moore, Campbell, Shelley, Wordsworth, Horne, Browning, Barrett, and Tennyson, as well as a separate sonnet, "The Old Masters," on Dante, Petrarch, and Michelangelo.[52] The long poem on English poets undoubtedly is either a rough or a final form of his "Heads of the Poets"; in it, Simms groups Tennyson, Robert Browning, Elizabeth Barrett, and R. H. Horne as writers who speak "For that fresh nature, which, in daily things,/ Beholds the immortal."[53] Of these Browning, although his power of poetic utterance was inferior to his thought, was probably considered the best, for in a review in 1850 Simms described him as "no common verse-maker. He is a writer of thought and genius, of peculiar and curious powers as an artist; subtle, spiritual, and singularly fanciful, and, though as yet perhaps unacknowledged, is one of the master minds of living European song. He is obscure, however, and will scarcely ever reach that degree of popularity which follows only the limpid and lucid. . . . When his peculiar phraseology shall become familiar to the ear, it will compel an admiration which is very far from general now."[54]

The English poet in the post-war years who roused his greatest interest was A. C. Swinburne. Simms was isolated from books, and on December 19, 1865, he wrote to E. A. Duyckinck to send him, among others, "a new Poem on the model of the Greek Drama, 'Somebody in Calydon,' of which I have heard loud mention."[55] Swinburne and Tennyson between them had even made long poems popular in magazines,[56] but his admiration for Swinburne's skill was more than counterbalanced by distaste for his tone. He noted perceptively, however, that "the prurience of passion, in these poems, is of a metaphysical sort, and is, for this reason, measurably harmless." Simms concluded that some of the verses in *Poems and Ballads* must have been written when Swinburne "was drunk"; in such earlier publications as *Atalanta in Calydon* he had shown himself admirably endowed, a flexible, elastic and lucid poet "even when most lofty in his flight."[57]

Although Simms had shown a similar moral bias earlier, it may be that Swinburne had simply come too late in his life for a just appreciation. He could find virtues in Horne's *Orion* and in Phillip James Bailey's *Festus* that elude the modern reader, although he was not blind to their faults;[58] he praised Sir Henry Taylor's *Artevelde* highly and linked his name with Tennyson as a great poet, but Hammond complained justly that his long article was a non-committal synopsis with copious quotations, written hastily to fill up that number of the *Southern Quarterly*.[59] Thomas Campbell and Thomas Moore he linked as appealing to readers in "our gentler moods," but not lifting the readers beyond beguilement they "leave us, where they found us."[60] Winthrop Mackworth Praed was even more a minor poet, but he was a man of fanciful and capricious fancy, who "mingles the fantastique and the grotesque with considerable felicity." He lived in an atmosphere of rhyme, and was a spontaneous singer, "always graceful, spirited, proper in sarcasm and sentiment, full of good sense. . . . He was as near to being a real poet as possible."[61] Thomas Hood was even better in presenting the contrasting "extremes of fun and pathos. . . . we have at his hands the most touching passages of sentiment, and the most quizzical bits of fun."[62]

Generally, Simms could find virtues in a poet's work to balance against the defects. A few times he was irritated or disgusted enough to write a blistering attack, without any attempt at mitigation; a representative and amusingly-phrased example is his blast at Martin Farquhar Tupper: "It is a 1,000 pities that a man who has such an 'alacrity in sinking' as Tupper, should not permit himself to subside quietly to the bottom . . . as happens frequently with a diseased oyster. . . . N. P. Willis had the honor of first fishing him up, and holding him out, limp and dripping to the American people. . . . Had he been content to rest on the laurels thus won, the Philosophy would still have kept its place on the tables of sentimental grocers and have furnished the inspiration of gushing school girls. Unfortunate Tupper! had you lived in the age of the Dunciad . . . Pope, with the instincts of genius, would have hailed you Prince of Grub-street."[63]

Simms' taste was mainly formed by nineteenth-century and Elizabethan poets. A voracious reader, he devoured the work of the major and many of the minor poets, of all periods; a constant reviewer, he commented energetically on any new editions of older poets that were sent to him. Moreover, he sprinkled allusions, quotations, and slight misquotations throughout his novels. When a very young soldier kills his first enemy, after describing his feelings, Simms added that he "looked the picture of the personification in the ode of Collins, where Fear—recoils, he knows not why,/ Even at the sound (wound) himself hath made."[64] An egotistical, addle-pated gallant "talked poetry by the canto and felicitated himself on the equal taste with which he enjoyed Butler and Cowley—the antipodes of English poets."[65] In his own right Simms in *Eutaw* takes a fling at "such geniuses as Pye, and Whitehead, and Warton, successively poets-laureate. We may judge readily of the sort of poets which could willingly sing the glories of the Guelphic dynasties of the Georges—first, second, or third."[66] In general, critical commentary is rare and incidental, for Simms was mainly drawing on poets for illustrative purposes.[67]

He also makes abundant use of quotations and allusions in non-fictional writing. In a single letter to James Lawson, Simms misquotes a Milton sonnet and a line from *Othello*, quotes from *Macbeth* and Samuel Johnson's "Vanity of Human Wishes" and from Milton's prose correctly, and has references to *As You Like It* and Ben Jonson.[68] He drew on Thomas Gray's "The Bard" and Oliver Goldsmith's "Elegy on the Death of a Mad Dog" with equal ease and fervor.[69] In his reviews, likewise, there are frequent comparisons and occasional critical asides. Although Wordsworth had no predecessor of equal genius, James Thomson "in his 'Seasons' had drawn admirable pictures of nature, but they were all injured by the somewhat extravagant diction of the period in which he wrote . . . they rather dazzle than please."[70] When his story "The Loves of the Driver" was attacked as vulgar and obscene, he quoted from the "Moral Poet" Alexander Pope, and noted that, along with such diverse writers as Shakspeare and Goldsmith, Pope had portrayed human beings so exactly and graphically that

even he "could not have escaped" nineteenth-century censor-
ship.[71] His respect for Pope as a serious professional poet,
and thus not kin to the artificial poetasters or gentlemanly
amateurs, he imbedded in an article on copyright.[72]

Usually his comments on Shakspeare and Dryden deal
with them as dramatists rather than directly as poets. Shakspeare's non-dramatic work, he thought, had "never yet been
properly examined . . . their analysis, from new points of
view, will probably make the reader acquainted with beauties
in them which few conceive them to possess." This analysis
would also reveal that the sonnets were in essence auto-
biographical: "They are more essential than all his dramas to
any just idea of the moral nature, and the temperament, of
their author."[73]

Milton's *Paradise Lost* was the touchstone by which he
judged contemporary epics and religious poems. As early
as 1828, he vigorously attacked Robert Pollok's *The Course
of Time* as consisting "neither of poetry nor verse," and
contrasted its feebleness with the "truly Epic grandeur" of
the older poem.[74] The scheme of Robert Montgomery's
Messiah he found vaster, more intricate, and more detailed
than Milton's, but his execution undramatic, inefficient, in-
coherent, and declamatory.[75] Although Montgomery's poem
was not successful artistically, it shared "the grand defect"
of most religious poems in that the author approached his
subject as an artist, without inspiration. But the great religious poet must have passions: "in the agonies of pain or
pleasure he finds utterance." In fact, the great poets, regardless of subject, "were all of them men of griefs and agonies."[76]
The religious poets write "not as a graceful exercise of the
mind . . . but because they are forced to do so, by the
struggling and striving feeling with them. . . . Its language
must be that of an emotion so deeply aroused and enkindled,
as to rise above all ordinary forms of expression."

Of relatively modern poets, only Milton and Dante
deserve to rank with such Old Testament poets as Job and
David. No human poet could succeed fully. In spite of the
grandeur of his theme, Milton could sustain himself, as
Montgomery could not: "That Milton is great, is rather
because he has not, and could not, have fallen so low as any
other human genius. That he is equal to his theme, unless

in a sense purely comparative, must be denied." This was an ideal judgment; when human and earthly standards were applied, *Paradise Lost* was clearly the best original religious poem in English.

In a sense, Simms' judgments were personal ones. But they were downright and honest. They were also based on wide and reasonably careful reading. Immediacy of appeal never led him to think or write of Wordsworth as a better poet than Milton. He never sharpened and rarely troubled to define his standards, but he did have certain criteria that as critic he undeviatingly held to. With these as touchstones, he decided upon and somewhat dogmatically delivered his personal judgments. Most of these have elements of validity in them; many are just and sensible; some are, truly, perceptive.

III

Friendships, prejudices, and enmities naturally played a greater part in Simms' treatment of American than of British poets. His allegiance was first of all to South Carolina; then to the South; finally to Philadelphia and New York. Although he became personally fond of some New Englanders and praised highly some New England writers, he seems never to have felt at home there, personally or intellectually. He was convinced that these writers possessed didactic rather than inventive powers; no mystic himself for all of his later interest in spiritualism, he believed that transcendentalism in America was mostly "balderdash, and very bad balderdash at that."[77] He would not have admitted to any prejudice; he was simply setting down the facts as they existed. Unorthodox himself, he approved of the ideas in Emerson's essays although he deprecated their "Carlyleisms"—not as underrating Carlyle, but as objecting to an American being "this or that Englishman's man." Although Emerson's essays in their content "declare a mind of his own," Simms preferred his poetry, as being "at once fresh, felicitous, and true."[78]

This was honest but in a sense qualified praise. There was no doubt in Simms' mind that William Cullen Bryant was the best of American poets. When his close friend James Lawson in 1839 wrote of "finding fault" with Bryant as a poet, Simms begged him, in terms that possibly over-stated somewhat his own beliefs, not to publish the essay: "I do not mean to say that he is faultless—for who can be?—but I must say I never met with a writer, ancient or modern—English or American so uniformly correct. Beware then, lest you suffer a difference of taste, to lead you to a false judgment. A difference of taste does not justify censure; and where you have to deal with one so perfect as Bryant, you should rather infer the things which do not please you, were not written for you, and not that they are censurable or unworthy . . . a boyish criticism of mine pronounced him the first American Poet, when, so far as my knowledge went, the judgment found no concurrence from any other quarter."[79]

In 1828 Simms had written that the *North American Review* and *American Quarterly Review* were unwise and uncritical in proclaiming Percival's "Ode to Seneca Lake" as superior to similar poems by Bryant and Byron. Percival's work is commonplace. Bryant's poems are not. He is, in fact, "justly ranked as the first of American poets," and his "chaste and beautiful productions would do honor to any age or country." In an editorial note, Simms adds that Bryant's merits and Percival's demerits are equally obvious.[80]

This was written before the two writers met in 1832; later they became friends and exchanged visits; just before and during the war the friendship was broken off; afterward, they became friends again. But Simms never changed in his critical judgment. Bryant in America was doing what Wordsworth did in England; he worked from the internal and moral idea to ally it with the external and physical world of nature; he was worthy of being compared with Wordsworth, though by no means the equal of the English poet. He wrote better blank verse than Cowper. Wordsworth and Cowper were in Simms' estimation rightfully among the masters; yet he did not hesitate to link Bryant's name with either of them.[81]

Simms' warmest personal tribute was published in 1842. In this essay he talks of their friendship, describes Bryant and his way of life, and of the times indoors and out that he has heard Bryant read poetry. Yet even in this personal tribute, Simms presented what he considered a just rather than a laudatory appraisal of the poet: after noting "the

exquisite polish of his poetry," Simms adds that his mind is
"rather discriminating than profound; his genius is manly
rather than bold, and we suspect that his fancy is somewhat
enfeebled by his fastidiousness. . . . He could never become
a passionate poet," partly because of a trait that deserved
high praise, the "delicacy of his tastes." Simms quoted the
newly-published "Antiquity of Freedom" with the comment that it "is distinguished by his usual characteristics—
a calm, contemplative philosophy . . . some forcible lines;
and conceptions rather bolder, in some instances, than those
which usually mark Mr. Bryant's writings."[82]

A few months later, in reviewing *The Fountain and
Other Poems*, he commends the "quiet, even-toned and
solemn sweetness, in the strains of Mr. Bryant," but laments
that this volume lacks any of "the grand Miltonic hymnings
of his previous publications." This was a defect; even so,
the book was good enough to prove again that Bryant
"is almost the only one of our poets, who does not give us
occasion to say that he writes too much."[83]

Possibly Simms' finest tribute to Bryant was written in
1859, after they had disagreed politically. It is also a fine
example of Simms' objectivity in judging literary works. The
Richmond *Enquirer* had published an editorial calling Bryant
"An Inditer of Mean Doggerel." To this Simms responded
vigorously: "We find Wm. Cullen Bryant referred to as
one 'whose vocation it is to write poetry without the inspiration, as a poor inditer of mean doggerel.'

"Now the express purpose of the editorial is the exposure
and denunciation of the political course of the New York
Evening Post—a most laudable object. . . . Why, should the
Editor of the *Enquirer* go out of his way to attack Bryant
the Poet, when his sole business is with Bryant, the black
Republican? Why should he make himself, at the outset of
his argument, supremely ridiculous by attempting to deny
the poetical claims of a man, whose fame was probably
established long before his wise critic was born?"[84]

In April, 1870, Simms wrote to Lawson that "Bryant
and myself have exchanged letters in the old vein, and the
entente cordiale is re-established between us."[85] On the basis
of extracts in *Putnam's Magazine*, Simms had written a notice
of Bryant's translation of *The Iliad*: "Mr. Bryant is not only

one of our best classical scholars, but he is also a master of classical *literature*. . . . His art has always been as nearly perfect as possible. He has been, what we properly style, a contemplative poet. But he has not been a wandering one; not easily led aside from Thought, by the attending Fancy."[86] Bryant lacked picturesqueness and sometimes warmth, but these minor defects only slightly impaired the excellence of his true and felicitous poetry.

Simms was personally fond of Fitz-Greene Halleck, describing him as a genial, humorous, witty person who "never forgot the gentleman in the poet."[87] In 1845 he seemed "one of our few classics." Simms defined the characteristics of his poetry, listing "its terseness, its felicitous turns of expression, its epigrammatic points, its adroit playfulnesses." His poetry depended for appeal on the mode of expression rather than the thought expressed. Although the thoughtful poet belonged to an entirely different and higher order, Simms noted that he was only attempting to place, without disparagement, Halleck's work, "for which we have very high esteem."[88] In a review in June, 1830, he had linked Bryant and Halleck as "among the very first metrical men of the country," noting that Halleck was a graceful writer who developed his individual works "with much polish and infinite judgment."[89] But even his best poems were "soon fathomed—they have no profundity. . . . Halleck, I suspect, lacks a high moral sense, and wit and humor form no necessary constituents of the poetical character—nay, I am inclined to think that they subtract from the earnestness of purpose and design, which, as much as any thing besides, leads to the effectual accomplishment of any very elevated poetical task."[90]

Halleck was far better than Joseph Rodman Drake, whose "Culprit Fay" struck him as "fanciful not imaginative—the measure is not good and the conceits not only stale but puerile." Drake deserved only a New York reputation, but Halleck for all his faults had been badly underrated throughout the country: in his special vein he was a true if minor poet.[91]

Simms had weighty misgivings about the value of Longfellow's work. It was "delicate, graceful, ingenious," but it was derivative, and limited by the "extreme simplicity" of his thought.[92] He considered Poe "more than half right" in accusing Longfellow of plagiarism[93] (possibly influenced by his affiliation with the "Young America" group and by his friendship with Evert Duyckinck), and as late as 1869 still thought that Longfellow, "who stole from everybody," in his tragedies had certainly "*gazed* upon" the *Witchcraft* of Cornelius Mathews. In his fury at this supposed theft Simms admitted that Longfellow "has been clever enough as an artist, to conceal his thievings. . . . Were L. as great a Poet as he is an artist, he might take Cowper by the hand. Dante would not suffer an introduction."[94] Many of Longfellow's shorter pieces were "tasteful and pretty," but they were essentially the work of "an adroit artist" who lacked "invention."[95] Occasionally they were powerful: "The Skeleton in Armor" he described as "a spirited Norse ballad by Longfellow which is a devilish sight more like poetry than his 'Blacksmith' stuff."[96]

He did not like the longer poems. *The Song of Hiawatha* seemed to him "dreary, irredeemable nonsense," and *Evangeline*, very little better, a "comparative failure." Yet "such of his verses as appeal to the affections, are household songs throughout the land. Upon these productions, rather than upon any of his elaborate efforts, we are convinced his fame must rest."[97] In spite of his great defects, Longfellow had earned this limited fame since, in the best of his lyrics and sonnets, for "purity, grace, sweetness, the consistency of tone, the charm of manner, the delicacy of his fancy, and the melody of his strain, it would be scarce possible to find his equal among living poets, and still more difficult to assert that he has any superior."[98]

James Russell Lowell, "more of a poet and less of an artist," was perhaps better. He was vigorous, fecund with thoughts and fancies, although too subservient to Boston opinion and too much given to fugitive works.[99] But Lowell gave Simms a chance to "pepper Yankeedom," and in two reviews of *A Fable for Critics* he made the most of this opportunity, complaining that Lowell had many "flings" at the South that were "mere impertinences, not called for by his subject, but lugged in by the head and shoulders," and these exhibit in the author "a bad, malicious heart." Lowell was better in his thoughtful and sentimental than in his satirical poems, although *A Fable* had some good as well as many bad points: "It is sharp and sometimes spicy, playful and fanciful, amidst much clumsiness and cumbrousness. But the fable is feeble, the point is not apparent, and the malice much more conspicuous than the wit."[100]

Whittier he objected to as the author of "offensive abolition poems," but he admitted that although declamatory in manner, they showed energy and life. Yet his talent was didactic rather than imaginative, and best suited for the occasional ode, which he successfully made into a "fierce lyric."[101]

Simms wrote to E. A. Duyckinck as late as December 30, 1855, that "I should like to know Holmes."[102] He felt that Holmes was humane in a way that Lowell and Whittier were not. Five years later, he found *The Professor at the Breakfast Table* a book to take up frequently and with pleasure, for the Professor is "discursive, oracular, thoughtful, playful, with a mixture of fancy and philosophy." Simms would like to have the Professor or his creator as a guest, "in order to enjoy the Professor's eloquence from his living mouth."[103] He liked Holmes' verse, although when he compared his own *City of the Silent* with Holmes' poem at the dedication of Pittsfield Cemetery, he thought his own work vigorous and imaginative, that of Holmes "feeble and commonplace."[104] This was not usually true. Most of Holmes' poems were "trenchant enough, but not ill-natured." Moreover, Simms had the highest respect for Holmes' technical skill: "The verse flows with great smoothness, is roughened with dexterity, so as to prevent monotony, and is full of vivacity."[105]

In 1853 Simms characterized George Henry Boker's poetry as "quaintly thoughtful and picturesque." He met Boker, liked him, and corresponded with him, although Simms' letters have not been located. Gradually he came to feel that Boker was the best writer of sonnets in the United States,[106] and in 1867 he stated sweepingly (perhaps only with sonnet-writing mainly in mind, since he was reviewing *The Book of the Sonnet*) that Boker was "the most really able, various and powerful of all the poets which the Northern States have produced."[107] This review surprised and pleased Boker, who had not expected to receive critical "justice" from such unreconstructed Southerners as Simms and Paul Hamilton Hayne. For Boker's fellow-Pennsylvanian, the "buoyant" Bayard Taylor, Simms had far less regard, although he enjoyed talking with him and reading his travel books; but Taylor's poetry exhibited neither profound emotions, nor deep thinking. It was "sweet and graceful throughout," for Taylor presented "well known sentiments in very felicitous phraseology," but it was picturesque surface poetry, excellent of its kind, but one got its full value on the first reading.[108]

Edgar Allan Poe had genius. Simms never doubted that. It was questionable, however, that Poe had wisely or completely employed his talents. Poe's mind was "curiously metaphysical and subtle," his imagination probing and daring,[109] but his genius was bizarre and he was, Simms feared, "too much the subject of his moods—not sufficiently so of principle." But he found Poe's writings "always interesting," although when Poe "contended for fugitive performances" he was only rationalizing "his own short comings."[110] But critics who tried to apply literary standards applicable to Dryden or Pope misunderstood and misjudged Poe's work. He did not help the reader with moral axioms or philosophical maxims; he demanded that the reader "surrender himself to influences of pure imagination." The reader who can yield himself will find a "severe symmetry," and a remarkable intensity: as in his stories, "How intensely he can pursue, to its close, a scheme of the imagination—imagination purely—rigidly defining his principles as he goes, step by step, and maintaining to the sequel, the most systematic combinations of proprieties and dependencies." Yet if Poe seemed notable chiefly for his use of imagination and intensity, he had also as characteristic qualities the "music of the verse, the vagueness of the delineation, its mystical character, and dreamy and spiritual fancies."[111] These were good qualities, but Poe's avoidance of the concrete, with his reliance on imagination and fancy, "wings his thoughts to such superior elevations, as to render it too intensely spiritual for the ordinary reader."[112]

The fact that Poe's poems and tales constituted a remarkable contribution to American literature did not make him a good model for other writers. "You show too greatly

how much Poe is in your mind," he complained to Thomas
Holley Chivers. As a poet Chivers had many good qualities:
poetic ardor, command of language and fluency of expression, skill in versification, delicacy of taste, and spirituality;
but, like Poe, he was willful and perverse.[113] *The Lost
Pleiad* (1845) had excellent poems in it, but suffered from
a monotony brought on by the author's writing too sub-
jectively of personal bereavement: "He allows the man constantly to interfere with and to thwart the objects of the
poet." Too much of his work was elegiac and individual,
written too immediately out of personal emotion. Chivers
was too good a poet to continue on "his present erroneous
career," he concluded sternly.[114] In 1852 and 1853, in a personal letter and in brief reviews, he again attempted to persuade Chivers away from subjectivity and mysticism, for
"You have too much real ability to be suffered to trifle
with yourself and reader."[115] Chivers was not grateful, but
in his turn accused Simms of having "a perfect *contempt*
for what may be called the Art of Composition."[116]

A major reason for being severe on able, gifed writers
grew out of Simms' great desire for a valid American and
Southern literature. His friend Cornelius Mathews had great
natural endowments; in two reviews of Mathews' poetry,
Simms notes his promise and his power, but perversely
Mathews "studies hard to wrong his talents" by over-indulg-
ing his liking for obscurity and a strained originality, and by
refusing to master the techniques of versification.[117] H. T.
Tuckerman with his "gentle, musical, and contemplative"
poetry revealed a mind "more tasteful than searching"; both
in his poetry and his essays Tuckerman needed "an occasional
painstaking roughening of the style."[118] Poets of a limited
accomplishment like Frances Sargent Osgood he was ready
to accept lightly, for in her fluent and exurberant verse, "free
from grave thoughts and deep philosophies," she was undoubtedly writing as well as she could.[119] It was different
with Mathews and probably with Tuckerman; it was different
with the remarkably gifted A. B. Meek of Alabama, who
lazily preferred to remain a dilettante instead of working to
become a first-rate poet.[120] Simms regretted especially the
untimely death of Philip Pendleton Cooke, for though "less
of the artist than Longfellow," he had "a far more active and

native fancy. . . . His original ballads have all the characteristics of Froissart, and of the Ballad mongers of his day."[121]

In Southern and especially in South Carolina writers Simms sought for qualities worth praising, and he recommended a generous patronage without too much regard for literary quality, since only by encouraging young authors could the region hope to develop a literature. If a sufficient number of able young men became writers, the quality of some of their work would undoubtedly be high.[122] In the meantime, he praised whenever possible the work of older Charlestonians like William Henry Timrod and William J. Grayson.[123] Athough he personally disliked and distrusted James Mathewes Legare, he praised the poems in *Orta-Undis* as "full of instances of rare felicity of phrase, happy turns of thought, analogies equally sweet and curious, and fine moralities that crown the verse, at its close, with a sudden surprise and beauty." Too often he had merely "caught up the overflow of his fancy," but that was delicate and sweet.[124] Washington Allston was a professional painter, and he had given serious attention to aesthetics: "his acknowledged familiarity with all those laws of taste which are equally essential to the proper direction of poet as well as painter, will necessarily make every syllable that he has written upon the subject of art, a word of weight." Simms could praise the "gentle, benign, and thoughtful" man; the painter and aesthetician; and the author of the novel *Monaldi*—from which he quoted copiously. But Allston definitely was "not a poet in the high, perhaps the only proper sense of the term. He was not an original thinker in verse,—not a seer,—not inspired. His poems are rather those of the accomplished and educated gentleman,—the man of taste and purity, of grace and sentiment, than the poet. . . . His intercourse with the muse is not one of passion. His amours are purely platonic."[125]

After 1850 Simms set his hopes in poetry mainly on his young friends Henry Timrod and Paul Hamilton Hayne. Sometimes they behaved like fractious nephews, disregarding the sound and competent advice he gave them; Timrod in particular did not always conceal his scornful impatience with Simms' Johnsonian pronunciamentos on poetry, although in a letter now lost he acknowledged that "Somehow or other, you always magnetize me on to a little strength."[126] As Hayne remembered it, there had never been a cloud of any kind on their relationship, but Simms in April 1857 was hurt because Hayne and John Russell, as editor and publisher of the newly-started *Russell's Magazine*, "have equally forgotten that such a person as myself exists. They have both sucked the orange and neither values the skin."[127] These were but temporary irritations. For his young friends Simms had a geniune liking and admiration.

Timrod was physically frail and morbidly sensitive. Unlike Simms, he wrote slowly, "with great pains-taking and labour." But he was indubitably "one of our truest and purest native poets";[128] he was not flexible, but he was "refined and highly polished, with fine meditative tone, and a pure and graceful fancy."[129] Simms rather tended to underrate the intellectual content in Timrod's poems on nature and the emotional feeling implicit in his war poems. Timrod had genius and artistry, but he "was not passionate; he was not profound; he laboured in no field of metaphysics; he simply sang . . . with a native gift, of the things, the beauties, and the charms of nature. He belonged, in the classification of literary men, to the order that we call the contemplative." Simms admired his skill in versification and "felicitous turns of thought and expression," so that "whether he sang of his own or the loves of others, the open purity of his genius refined equally the thought which he expressed and the verse in which he clothed it."[130]

Hayne had certain virtues that Timrod lacked. Hayne was friendly and cheerful; he showed a more open-hearted admiration of Simms; in fact, of all the young South Carolina writers, Hayne became Simms' closest and dearest friend. Moreover, he was industrious, and Simms thought that "Industry will tell even in so poor a profession as literature, which is hardly a profession in so poor a world of art as ours."[131] Hayne's greatest defect was that he *"deliberately sat down to manufacture a long series of provocative and exciting events into lyrics,"* instead of writing out of inspiration, imagination, and passion. This revealed a mistake on Hayne's part as to the nature of the lyric, which should be an unpremeditated overflowing of the poet's spirit. Simms complained of this somewhat mechanical quality in Hayne's poem on poets, "The Southern Lyre," although generally it was "a very felicitous performance, chaste, graceful, fanciful, and very happily versified throughout. You have done singularly well in handling a subject, which required very nice skill, discrimination, tact, and the appreciation of effects and characteristics."[132]

But his long three-part review[133] of Hayne's *Avolio* (1860) is disappointing. He excuses himself for having postponed the review because "the popular mind alternates between a sweat and a stew!" His own mind was absorbed by politics; but seizing "a moment of respite—from political pressure," he wrote a somewhat perfunctory analysis of Hayne's work. Some praise is freely given, qualified by much heavy-handed advice. At his best Hayne "soars as well as sings. . . . He possesses, indeed, a variety of notes, some of them of large compass—all of them sweet and musical, and many of them no less vigorous and passionate than fanciful and rich." But over-use of the Fancy makes his poetry too voluptuous and ornate; and Hayne erred grievously, Simms thought, in trying to write sensuous love poems in the sonnet form. Simms preferred the longer narrative poems as being more finished and more delicately told. Somewhat oddly, he recommended that Hayne in the future cast his love poems in the form of ballads, and that he concentrate on long historical narratives in verse. Perhaps fortunately, Hayne largely disregarded this avuncular advice.

In his *War Poetry of the South* (1867), Simms included practically all of the best war poems of Timrod and Hayne, with a generous selection of his own work. These represented, he was convinced, the best work done by Confederate poets. He undertook the work primarily because of the "goad of that necessity which makes money so precious to me at this moment";[134] the selecting and editing were done hastily, but even so the task entailed a heavy correspondence and a difficult job of selection. He was especially pleased to be able to present the work of many men whom he valued as friends even more highly than as poets; he went to considerable effort to see that S. Henry Dickson, J. Dickson Bruns, William J. Grayson, John Esten Cooke, John R. Thompson, Margaret Junkin Preston, James Barron Hope, James Ryder Randall, Francis O. Ticknor, A. B. Meek, and A. J. Requier were fairly represented. These were minor poets, but within rather strait limits he thought them valid and authentic versifiers, and at times truly poets, though under the stress of emotion they were "speaking out with a passion which disdains subterfuge, and through media of imagination and fancy, which are not only without reserve, but which are too coercive in their own nature, too arbitrary in their influence, to acknowledge any restraints upon that expression, which glows or weeps with emotion. . . . With this persuasion, we can also forgive the muse who, in her fervor, is sometimes forgetful of her art."[135]

Actually, it did not require war-time emotions for Simms to set fervor, power, content, and thought above artistry. The bold and striking idea was to him more important than the form in which it was expressed. As critic, he naturally favored those poets who presented ideas that he approved. Sometimes he rode his prejudices hard. Yet it was his intention always, as he wrote to H. T. Tuckerman, "to dispense just judgment," and he was pleased when a living author professed himself satisfied.[136] But an individual's satisfaction was of minor importance. What mattered was to establish an intellectual climate in which good writing would be widely and generously recognized. Believing as he did in the ultimately practical value of poetry, Simms thought such a climate essential to the health of a nation and a people. In his own time, the best way in which a critic might contribute to this development was by "puting on record," honestly and vigorously, his own personal beliefs about poets and poetry.

CHAPTER IV

On Dramas and Dramatists

THAT Simms greatly enjoyed attending and reading plays has been frequently noted. On one occasion he wrote that he and his wife would go from the plantation "to town [Charleston] . . . as sooon as we hear of the arrival of Mrs. Kean [Ellen Tree]" and of her husband Charles.[1] Six weeks later he reported to the same correspondent that "we saw the Keans with a great deal of pleasure."[2] These comments are typical. So is the inclusion in a single order for books of a ten-volume edition of the works of Beaumont and Fletcher, and of the Alexander Dyce editions of Christopher Marlowe and George Peele.[3]

This interest in the drama, especially the Elizabethan, was intensely personal, yet it was also in part professional. In April, 1841, he wrote to the editor and publisher George Roberts that, in preference to writing a novel, "My *penchant* is for another field very different from that in which I am more generally known to the public; and I will avail myself of the earliest leisure to send you a specimen of Dramatic Composition."[4] Although his faith in his prowess as dramatist proved misguided, it did not die quickly or easily. Over three years later, he wrote to his friend James Lawson that "I am more and more inclined to the conviction that I am to prove my fate in the drama. We must have [Edwin]Forrest at our conference, for I am determined if I can to make him my colleague in glory."[5]

The hoped-for glory never became a reality. Forrest never produced a play by Simms, although from the somewhat contradictory evidence he seems to have accepted and per-haps earlier to have suggested an adaptation of *Timon of Athens*, for Simms wrote to Lawson: "I shall cover to you by next Saturday's steamer, a packet to Forrest containing the first two acts of Timon of Athens, as I have altered it for him. . . . I have endeavored to conform as much as possible to his and your suggestions, and have been as brief in my dialogue as was consistent with the plan of the piece and the necessities of the action. In the same packet are the two copies of the play which he lent me; and which, as I have the dramas, I shall no longer need." Even after the adaptation had been completed, Forrest was dilatory, first about acknowledging receipt of the manuscript and then about revising it: "he tells me he has not yet studied, or even cut and arranged the piece." Although Forrest kept the manuscript for several years, he never produced the play, and Simms never published it.[6]

This enthusiasm for writing plays is a bit surprising, for in general Simms believed in the superiority of the modern novel as being more "pliant in the hands of the master, it is more universal in its appreciation of the desires of the multitude. . . . To its influence may be ascribed, in part, the decline of the drama in popular estimation."[7] Simms had no desire to write closet dramas, any more than he desired to write novels that would not sell; if Forrest and other producers would not bring out his plays, he wrote in 1847, he would salvage what he could: "I will make a volume of my Arnold, Michael Bonham, Locrine, Atalantis and adding this 'man of the people,' close my account with the Dramatic World in a single publication."[8] But in the same letter Simms promises that if Forrest finds Norman Maurice playable, he will come to New York and make the necessary revisions. Forrest was not interested and Simms complained bitterly that "I can't afford to work to keep my MSS in their pigeon holes."[9]

As critic of his own plays, Simms was aware of certain weaknesses and defects. The known facts of history, in particular, cramped his imagination. With Michael Bonham he admitted that he had taken a few liberties, "but the history will suffer little from my freedoms, while, I believe, the story gains by them.[10] But near the end of the hand-written introductory essay to Benedict Arnold: The Traitor. A Drama in an Essay, he confesses that frequently he "was baffled by the details of history. I had no sufficient freedom. . . . I was stopt by stern barriers of fact, such as do not oppress us in the ancient histories."[11]

He also had difficulties with dramatic style. When Forrest complained that *Norman Maurice* was not "carefully elaborated," Simms defended his work (in a letter to their friend James Lawson): "this moderation of tone was deliberately determined on, in consequence of my wish to make the piece strictly a *domestic* drama. The style was just sufficiently elevated to make it meet the exactions of rhythm. If the piece has any dramatic susceptibilities—if, in other words—it can be made a good *acting* piece, it will be quite easy to raise the style where it is necessary, and to throw in those extraneous passages of poetry, which I rather suppressed in order that it should be strictly an acting drama."[12]

Yet, amazingly for Simms, he was forced to admit that the action lagged, for "the situations are not sufficiently frequent in the 2 first acts," although he thought the closing scene of the second act "an effective one." But the characters and motivation seemed to him sound: these "might be heightened, strengthened," but they ought not to be fundamentally changed.[13]

Undoubtedly Forrest thought that *Norman Maurice* could not be sufficiently improved to be worth producing. However, there may have been some personal feeling involved. In *Border Beagles* (1840, p. 80), Simms describes a young actor imitating "Kean, excelling in the spasmodic hoarseness of his utterance—in the fury of the Pythia without her inspiration—now the lugubrious whinings of Cooper, when declining toward the fifth act; and now the gutteral growl of Forrest, when, with singular bad taste, he imitates even the death-rattle in the throat of the obese Vitellius."[14] Criticism of this kind was not likely to be forgotten or forgiven; at the time, Forrest and James Lawson were so offended that Simms was driven to protest: "I trust that you believe I think scarcely less highly of Forrest's genius than you do yourself; but I like to be a discriminate admirer. I thought and still think that he errs in taste when he avails himself of a feature so revolting, and in such cases, so unnatural, as this in connection with his death upon the stage." Simms within a fortnight had persuaded himself that his "references to Forrest, however critical, are in truth complimentary,"[15] but it seems exceedingly doubtful that the actor could have been converted to this view.

Yet part of Simms' difficulties may have been caused by a fundamental difference in point of view. The managers have made a basic mistake in selecting and shaping plays for the critics rather than the audience. In the United States, as in Shakspeare's time, "the success of the drama will once more depend upon addressing it *to the people and not to the critics.*" The critics are interested in comparing actors in various roles, or in comparing presentations; but most people go for the story. They are more interested in the play than in the actor.[16] Chiefly for that reason, "theatricals cannot well be said to flourish in New York. They rather live, like the variety of other amusements found here, by toleration and the chance custom yielded by transient persons."[17]

II

With some justice, William P. Trent asserts that Simms thought he had solved his own dramatic problem "by combining a strictly American plot with a method of presentation taken at second hand from his favorite Elizabethans."[18] Hugh Holman extends this observation, though more charitably, to Simms' practices in his novels; he demonstrates persuasively that "Simms borrowed at least a part of his method for presenting his characters from the English drama. . . . [his] debt to English drama did not consist solely in his use of dramatic means for the presentation of characters; it is also apparent in his use of the 'humours' character, as it was evolved by Ben Jonson and employed by the Jacobean and Restoration playwrights."[19] Frances M. Barbour argues that the well-known trial of Occonestoga for treason in *The Yemassee* (Ch. XXV) is derived from or at least suggested by Nathaniel Lee's poetic drama, *Lucius Junius Brutus,* for both emphasize death as preferable to dishonor.[20]

Simms probably knew Lee's play, although he does not mention that writer in his extant letters. But he preferred the earlier dramatists. This is indicated by his remark . that "Porgy, before entering the army, was well read in Shakspeare, Milton, Dryden, and the best of the then-current authors. It must be admitted, we fear, that he had also drank freely of fountains less undefiled; had dipped largely into the subsequent pages of the Wycherlys, the Vanbrughs, the

Congreves, the Wilmots, Ethereges, and Rochesters, of a far less intellectual, and therefore less moral, period."[21] Grace W. Whaley has shown Simms' preference by tabulating the quotations in eighteen of his novels: of the 306 quotations, 120 are from Shakspeare; 17 from unidentified old plays; 8 from Beaumont and Fletcher; 8 from Massinger; 7 from Jonson; 7 from Shirley; 6 from Middleton; 4 from Webster; 3 from Heywood; 3 from Chapman; 2 from Marlowe. Yet she deliberately omits *Border Beagles,* on the reasonable ground that the "plot of that novel calls for many quotations from Shakespeare."[22]

An important character in it is a young, naive, good-hearted, and unemployed Shakspearean actor. Tom Horsey is obsessed with Shakspeare. Although poor, he had acquired the editions of "Gifford, Malone, Steevens, Seymour, Rowe, Farmer, and some thirty or forty more" and kept them on the table by his couch;[23] as noted earlier, he could imitate the well-known actors of his day; he constantly quoted from the plays. So obsessed was he that once in his sleep he spoke and in part acted out long passages from *Romeo and Juliet;*[24] on another occasion, he begins by disputing the correctness of Forrest's reading of two lines from *Macbeth* and becomes so engrossed in his vigorous recital of favorite passages that he overturns a dug-out. In the words of his discomfited companion, "That putting out of the candle did the trick."[25]

As presented by Simms, Horsey is a comic but not an undignified figure. He is capable of believing that a gang of outlaws are unemployed actors "almost playing gipsy in the swamp to save expense"; he is easily seduced into believing that the state will subsidize a great Mississippi Shakspearean and Thespian Company; but he is capable also of taking a manful part in capturing the outlaws. His over-enthusiasm had improved him in some ways, but it had robbed him not only of commonsense but of discrimination: "He was one of those profound devotees of the great literary outlaw, who venerates his very faults, even as the antiquarian treasures up the rust and canker of the relic."[26]

This love of quotation and allusion is readily apparent in Simms' letters. In one, he quotes from *The Tempest,* compares the recipient to Caliban, and welcomes him "among us Benedictines."[27] A newly-married man is frequently referred

to as a Benedict; a cold-blooded villain as an Iago (or sometimes, drawing on Goethe, as a "cold demon Mephistopheles");
one growing fat as like Falstaff. The allusions are always appropriate and frequently humorous, but the quotations and
ascriptions are not impeccable. He frequently quoted or
paraphrased John Home's line (*Douglas*, I, i) to describe a
pregnant woman: "As women wish to be who love their lords."
But he ascribed the line to Shakspeare.[28]

When his retentive memory betrayed him, he did not
readily admit error. In *Beauchampe* (1856, p. 118), he quoted
four lines from Dekker, but attributed them to Middleton;
ten years later, in a letter to Hayne, Timrod wrote that "Mr.
Simms has in more than one place attributed that passage to
Middleton. I have assured him over and over again that he was
mistaken, but to no purpose. Please show him, when you next
meet, the passage in the last scene of the 1st Part of 'The
Honest Whore.' "[29]

When a passage or word was disputed, Simms argued
vigorously for his own preferences. Thus, some American
editions gave Pistol's speech in *The Merry Wives of Windsor*
(I. iii): "He hath studied her well, and translated her will—
out of honesty into English." Simms paraphrased this in order
to present more forcefully what he believed the proper reading: "You have read her will,—her wish—the secret desires of
her mind—She wills all that you intimated—She is secretly
the lecher you describe etc. A play upon words is suggested
by the use of the one in question, and Shakspeare was not the
author to lose any such opportunity. Then, while the American
editions make sense of the sentence, and what is esteemed very
good common sense too, it does not make the sense of Pistol,
nor the sense of Shakspeare,—that occult two-fold signification
which was in both their minds."[30]

Simms published only a few of his proposed emendations,
although he noted that in "my desk copy of Shakspeare, I find
I have . . . covered the pages of the immortal Bard with
notes."[31] Mainly the published notes were based on what
seemed to him simply common sense. He had personally
suffered from typographical errors; he was convinced that
similar errors marred the text of Shakspeare. In *The Tempest*,
the printers had a meaningless line, "Urchins shall for that
vast of night." This was simply a matter of incorrect spacing;

the line should read "Urchins shall *forth at* vast of night."[32]
A "frequent typographical error," the printing of *ere* for *e'er*,
had given rise to even more frequent critical notes, as had
the simple substitution of an O for a B: clearly "Out 3 years
old" should be "But three years old." Sometimes the error
could not be clearly resolved. When Alonzo addressed the
Boatswain, "Where's the master? Play the men," either of
two readings seemed to him "reasonable": "He encourages
the one in command, in their extremity, to ply his men and
keep their courage and perseverance from abatement, or
[Play the Man] he thus incites him to the performance of
his own duty."

But he objected to emendations and word-changes based
on modern usage, when they were quite understandable in
their Elizabethan meanings. Shakspeare's choice of words
was usually better than that of his editors. Dr. Johnson
quibbled over the word *behavior* when his own Dictionary
justified its definition as *conduct*. Discussing *King John*, Simms
argues that there is no need for Steevens' note on a speech
by Queen Elinor (Act I, Scene i) about Philip's father: "He
hath a trick of Coeur-de-Lion's face." Trick simply meant
likeness, and its meaning was readily apparent. The com-
mentators too often forgot that a passage like this first scene
was written entirely for acting, and on the stage becomes "not
only intelligible enough, but really forcible." A more serious
objection could be lodged against the characterization at the
end of the play: "I am not satisfied with the fidelity of a
character, like the Bastard, to a weak, capricious, and heart-
less tyrant such as he knows John to be."[33]

He commented frequently on new editions, and was willing
to accept the newly discovered Folio of Collier as authentic,
although he admitted that Richard Grant White had made
"sundry good and judicious objections" to it.[34] But he was
roused to wrath by the attempts of Delia Bacon and Nathaniel
Holmes to prove that the plays were written by Lord Bacon.
Holmes rides boldly forward, "like a very knight of the school
La Mancha, throwing down his windmill giants." He is fertile
in argument and suggestion, but "the very grounds upon which
he would assign the works of Shakspeare to Francis Bacon, are
not only conclusive that *he* (Bacon) did not write them, but
that he *could not* have written them."[35]

In his own estimation, Simms' most important single work on Shakspeare was a four-part article, "The Moral Character of Hamlet," which he later expanded and used frequently as one or as two lectures. "I flatter myself," he wrote to Lawson, "that I unlock the whole mystery of Hamlet's character and conduct."[36]

Simms begins the article by noting that of the master dramatists of Shakspeare's time, only Ben Jonson wrote for readers as well as for spectators; only his mind was imbued with the ancient dramatic rules, and his genius trained by a close study of them. All the other writers, in the infancy of English dramatic art, were careless and inconsistent, with that "natural outlawry of mood which is the invariable characteristic of superior genius."[37] Since Elizabethan plays were meant for the stage, not for printing, the "highest finish" of art was not much regarded; propriety was less important than securing and holding attention; and the dramatists worked in strong passions, unfettered by "restraints of form and delicacy."[38]

He cited two examples of what he considered a disregard of the proprieties and consistencies in *Hamlet*: Laertes in the beginning is an excellent and chivalrous gentleman, but in the end he is "one of the basest and most loathsome" of villains; Hamlet in Act I is a mere college youth, but in Act V he is thirty and his philosophical reflections are those of a man. Yet the action of the play is not over thirty days. Audiences would not be aware of such blemishes; readers are.[39]

Ironically, these minor defects occur in one of Shakspeare's finest plays and best-delineated persons, for Simms regarded the "moral character of Hamlet, not only as one of the noblest studies of Shakspeare's genius, but as one of the most perfect and symmetrical—a character every way natural."[40]

After reviewing the earlier interpretations of critics and editors (and in part disagreeing with practically all of them), Simms presents his own beliefs.[41] Hamlet, like Macbeth, was a victim of the fates; each was singled out for an ordeal to which he proved unequal, and he perished because of his unfitness. Hamlet's education, his training as a gentleman, and his temperament had deprived him of toughness and unfitted him for action, so that misfortune and danger brought out his nervousness, intensified his natural suspiciousness and indecisiveness. In a crisis his irresolution rendered useless all the natural endowments of his genius. Since Hamlet had never been properly trained for action, he tries to avoid "the necessity imposed upon him by the command of the ghost"; since he was by nature contemplative, he must be roused to action by an external force.[42]

Even so, he delays. He shams lunacy, but this is "simply a disguise, worn when it suits him, and cast off at a moment's warning."[43] Although he has no doubt that his father has been murdered and his uncle is guilty, he rationalizes on the nature of the ghost in order to gain time and to nerve himself to action, for his metal "rings hollow under the stroke of danger." His professed desire that Claudius' soul go to hell is spoken only by his lips, as part of his effort to force himself to act; not by his head or heart, for he is actually unwilling to kill his uncle. Eventualy he does act, athough in violation of his nature.[44]

The article ends abruptly, but in the manuscript of the second lecture Simms summarizes briefly: "The moral of Hamlet's character lies in its own weakness. It is important to lay this bare, as it so happens that the frequent moral beauty of his sentiments have led to a too favorable estimate of his own moral. . . . With all his infirmities, there is much in the character of Hamlet to commend him to our sympathies."

III

Simms had a fondness for grouping writers within a certain category. Thus he believed that the English spirit by nature was essentially tragic rather than comic or humorous. To prove this he cited mainly dramatists: "It is to the writings of Milton and Shakspeare, Beaumont and Fletcher, Massinger and Marlowe, rather than those of Farquhar and Congreve, and Vanbrugh and Cibber, that the English trace their intellectual supremacy."[45] He also set great value on the story as story. In a discussion of the novel, he included among the world's great story-tellers Shakspeare, Marlowe, Beaumont and Fletcher, Peele, Greene, Dekker, and Jonson.[46] He listed most of these, and added Shirley, as among the writers who have employed the deadly sins of man as well as his virtues, in great and moral works of literature—this in his attempt to refute charges of immorality against his story, "The Loves of the Driver." Massinger in particular did him yeoman service, for he quotes a long, apt, and effective passage on literary morality from one of his "most noble tragedies," *The Roman Actor.*[47]

Near the end of his long, semi-dramatic poem "Caius Marius," Simms deliberately paralleled or unconsciously imitated Ben Jonson. The echo seems deliberate; at any rate, Simms called attention to it in a footnote: "The reader will be reminded by this passage of that noble and solemn speech made by the Ghost of Sylla, at the opening of Ben Jonson's tragedy of Catiline: 'Dost thou not feel me, Rome,' etc."[48]

Apparently the one later dramatist he considered worthy to rank with the Elizabethans was John Dryden. *All For Love* was a remarkably fine drama; Dryden was in this play "an avowed imitator of Shakspeare—and his powers of imitation were wonderful—in respect to vigor of style, and a manly, energetic, and appropriate utterance in simple, direct and proper language, he is not unworthy of his model. . . . We need not say how little Dryden's genius possessed of the subtlety, spirituality, flexibility of Shakspeare, his melodious varieties and the depth and grandeur of his conceptions. But avoiding all comparison with the great master, the genius of Dryden was very noble, his learning great, and he merits far more consideration from the literary student than is now accorded him. A course of Dryden, after Milton and Shakspeare, would be useful."[49] His admiration extended to Dryden's criticism, for he recommended to a young writer that after acquainting himself with the "standard literature of the Shakspeare and Baconian period," he should then "not overlook the prose of Milton and the prefaces of Dryden."[50]

IV

Clearly *Othello* was one of his favorite plays. It was "one of the most noble of all dramatic moralities." He frequently quoted from it and alluded to various characters. After war broke out, he wrote to James Henry Hammond that, because there was no demand for his writing, "Othello's occupation is gone for the present"—a phrase which apparently haunted his mind, for he played changes on it in several others letters.[51] But his most striking and unconventional commentary is made

through the first-person narrator of *Confession;* although it
may not express Simms' own belief, it seems likely that he was
struck by certain contrasts between Othello and his own pro-
tagonist. Edward Clifford differentiates between them, and
attempts to define jealousy: "Mine was eminently a jealous
heart. On this subject of jealousy, men rarely judge correctly.
They speak of Othello as jealous—Othello, one of the least
jealous of all human natures! Jealousy is a quality that needs no
cause. It makes its own cause. It will find or make occasion
for its exercise, in the most innocent circumstances. The
proofs that made Othello wretched and revengeful, were
sufficient to have deceived any jury under the sun. He had
proofs. He had a strong case to go upon. It would have influenced any judgment. He did not seek or find these proofs
for himself. He did not wish to find them. He was slow to
see them. His was not jealousy. His error was that of pride
and self-esteem. He was outraged in both. His mistake was in
being too prompt of action in a case which admitted of deliberation. This was the error of a proud man, a soldier, prompt
to decide, prompt to act, and to punish if necessary. But never
was human character less marked by a jealous mood than
that of Othello. His great self-esteem was, of itself, a sufficient security against jealousy."[52]

Trent wrote that the "*motif* of 'Confession' seems to have
been a desire on Simms' part to rival Shakespeare in his greatest
play," and blames this on his "dabbling in morbid psychology."
Thus Simms was blind to the fact that Iago's practicing on
Othello excites our sympathy for the deluded hero, whereas
Clifford "excites our loathing and contempt." Although Trent's
personal judgment is here turned into an unqualified and rather
dubious series of generalizations, there seems no doubt that
Simms constantly had *Othello* in mind as he wrote *Confession.*[53]

Some of his key ideas on drama are embedded in his commentary on a weak contemporary play, *The Politicians,* by
Cornelius Mathews. In this play, the characters are uniformly
commonplace, vulgar, and deficient in dignity. Such names as
Brisk, Gudgeon, and Botch hint at this, but there are no names
that suggest a contrast. Not only is there nothing attractive
in the bill of fare, complains Simms; there is nothing natural
in the combination. Good comedy delineates various aspects

of society as it is, with many common, some vulgar, and at least a few noble persons. The "best works of Congreve, Cumberland, and Geo. Colman" prove this, but the best example is Shakspeare's *Merry Wives of Windsor*: "a story from humble life avowedly, yet with such an admixture of the high with the humble, the several constituencies of society in such combination—as we find ordinarily in society, and by which that curious moral amalgam is kept from becoming utterly monotonous and wretched. . . . The quick instincts of the dramatic veterans of the days of Elizabeth, led them at once to perceive that any unmixed representation of inferiority—not to say vulgarity—must really defeat the purposes of satire, no less than comedy."[54]

Mathews had failed also in his handling of dialogue: "His characters speak little essays. The one suggests a text to the other, which moves him to descant; and, instead of so speaking and acting as to hurry forward the action, they dilate on casual matters, deal in analyses of their neighbors and the opposite party, and waste time in dialogue which should be spent in action." Although these little essays read well, they make the play too explicit, so that the author "leaves nothing to the doubts and apprehensions of the spectator. It is the great characteristic of poetry in general, and the drama in especial, that language should be suggestive rather than full. Something must be left to the imagination of the audience. The clue must be put into their hands, and they left to follow it; and it is because of the actual part which they thus are made to take in the progress of events, that the drama forms an intellectual exercise much more exciting than any other which mortal genius has yet been able to conceive."[55]

V

In spite of his undoubted interest in the drama, Simms did not include any of his dramatic essays in his books, and he edited only one book that relates directly to the drama. W. P. Trent devotes only a scant half-paragraph to the book, dismissing the editor's work as "slight both in quantity and quality," although adding that Simms "undertook the task as a labor of love." Simms' letters indicate that he soon found that he had to spend "many tedious hours . . . in revising imputed plays of Shakspeare, a wearisome task which I am almost sorry to have undertaken." In his own judgment, he had done a good job, but the project "has cost me immense labor."[56]

Shakspearean scholars have set little value on Simms' editorial work on the Shakspeare Apocrypha.[57] The most recent editor of the apocryphal plays, C. F. Tucker Brooke, lists all of Simms' textual conjectures in his footnotes, and discusses some of the more and some of the least plausible ones in the section of notes after the plays.[58] Brooke dismisses most of these rather cavalierly and with some justice, for Simms lacked the scholarship and the books to handle textual problems adequately. He does not describe Simms' method, but it is easily discernible: Simms selected as his basic text the work of Charles Knight for *The Two Noble Kinsmen* and *A Yorkshire Tragedy*, and the edition of Malone for the five other plays. But he was no slavish follower. He levied upon Theobald, Seward, Mason, and Weber for emendations and for variant readings which he gave in footnotes; and he did not hesitate to make changes of his own, although he was scrupulous about noting all of these.

He mentions explicitly one change in *The Two Noble Kinsmen* about which he had consulted Knight: in II, 3, he makes Arcite's speech read   "and run,—

Swifter the wind upon a field of corn

(Curling the wealthy ears) ne'er flew."

Simms wrote of this: "with Mr. Knight's permission, I have ventured to restore the reading of *the* for *than*, with a new punctuation, preferring, though with great deference, the present construction to his own."[59] He was a modest editor, and as far as .conjectures and variants go, a reliable one.

Unfortunately Simms accepted Knight's expurgations and bowdlerized on his own hook, with the excuse that "Our edition is for general readers, as well as for critical students. The essential difference between Shakspeare and Fletcher makes it necessary to adopt a different course with reference to the two writers. It is not a false reverence for Shakspeare that calls upon an editor to leave his text unchanged; but a just discrimination between the quality of what is offensive in him and in other writers of his age. . . . I see no reason to disturb the opinions or depart from the rule that Mr. Knight has prescribed for himself, in the exclusion of offensive pas-

sages."⁶⁰ Although he believed *Locrine* to be by Shakspeare,
he does not hesitate to omit "simple" or "offensive" grossness.
In III, 4, he stops William's speech:
"Marry, Sir, what reason had you when my
sister was in the barn to—"
omitting the words
"tumble her upon the haie, and to fish her belly."⁶¹
The expurgations are carefully noted in all the plays, but they
make the texts worthless for the critical student or the general
reader. In accepting the custom of his own day the editor
limited this part of his work to that day.

His critical introductions should not be dismissed so lightly.
They have continuing interest, and some value, for they present an examination of the plays from the point of view of an
experienced creative writer.

Simms' exclusions are severe. He accepted for his book
only the seven plays "which have (wholly or in part) been
ascribed to his pen, and included, at an early period, among
his works." But he was not unmindful of the claims advanced
in later times "by ingenious criticism" for the inclusion of
other plays, and he half-promises that a group of these, "the
ascription of which to William Shakspeare rests chiefly upon
opinion," might be the matter for an additional volume. It was
never published, and presumably never edited. But Simms'
brief judgments upon these plays are worth quoting, as much
for what he voluntarily reveals of his own ignorance as of his
critical opinion. This group of excluded plays "comprises
'Arden of Feversham'—a piece of considerable merit; 'the
reign of King Edward III.'—a work so like Shakspeare's, in the
respects of versification and manner, that it is difficult to hit
upon any writer who could so happily have imitated him;
'George a-Greene, the Pinner of Wakefield'—which is now
supposed to have been written by Robert Greene, but upon
the most slender of all sorts of evidence; 'Fair Emma' [*sic*]—
which Mr. Knight assigns to a period subsequent to the death
of Shakspeare; 'Mucedorus,' of which we know nothing and
can express no opinion,—Tieck and Horn, the German critics,
pronounce it a youthful production of Shakspeare; Mr. Knight
gives us a brief analysis of the story, describes it as a lively
play, with some few passages of merit, but, otherwise, speaks
of it slightingly;—'The Birth of Merlin'—which in its first

known edition, that of 1662, was announced as the joint production of Shakspeare and Rowley; and 'The Merry Devil of Edmonton'—a performance which, as Mr. Knight justly remarks, is that of a true poet, whoever he may be."[62]

Simms' approach to the authenticity of individual plays was also conservative, but his approach to the general problem was bold and original. He had received little formal education, and no training in scholarship. But he had read widely and studiously, especially in the field of the Shakspearean drama, and he had made for himself a reputation as a distinguished novelist, a capable poet, and a vigorous critic. Aware of his own shortcomings, he was also aware of his achievements. His approach, then, was that of the creative writer, not that of the scholar; although he recognized the immense superiority of Shakspeare, he felt that the greater author had in his time surmounted many of the problems that he himself had once faced and only partially solved.

From that point of view, Simms is willing to admit that a youthful genius may turn out much bad work: "We have said that the deficiency of these works . . . is by no means to be admitted as an argument against their legitimacy. The opinion is not entertained without serious deliberation. The truth is, that a young author seldom writes from himself at first. He is more apt to write like anybody but himself. He subdues and suppresses himself. He does not feel himself. He is compelled to look out of himself for models and authorities, before he can properly unfold himself. . . . This very unfolding of self is the great business of life—never wholly effected, even with the utmost diligence, until the author has reached the mellow period of middle life, and seldom even then."[63]

Out of his own experience Simms was convinced that even the youthful Shakspeare was both imitative and derivative. He thought it a sufficient test of worth if he could find in a play by a very young man "an occasional germ which betrays freshness." But Simms' idea of just how young the author of some pieces may have been is a bit breath-taking. He was convinced that Shakspeare may have started writing by the time he was fifteen or sixteen, and that he had completed *Locrine* and *Titus Andronicus* by the time he went to London, "in his twenty-third year."

Simms' reasoning is at least plausible. The poetic germ,

he notes, usually takes virulent hold upon a potential writer
in his fifteenth year; although we do not know that Shakspeare
started that early, it would be "a strangely unreasonable sup-
position" to believe that a man so prolific in his later career led
a "vegetable life in Stratford." Here Simms drew upon his
own experience. At the age of eight he was celebrating in
verse the American victories over the British in the War of
1812, and according to his biographer "his pen was rarely
idle, and his brain never"; his first book was published when
he was nineteen; Trent suspects that many other youthful
effusions found a place in later volumes, and a play was about
this time accepted, rehearsed, and announced, although never
produced. But Simms knew that his own early work was
derivative: he was echoing the thoughts of others instead of
speaking his own mind.[64] He may well have thought he was
being very conservative when he suggested fifteen or sixteen
as a likely age for the composition of *Locrine* or other
apocryphal plays.

Simms draws a clear line between the plays that the boy
Shakspeare might have written, and those which are the work
of a mature person. The tests to be applied are entirely different. *A London Prodigal* is crude "as a work of thought
and as a work of art." It is the work of an apprentice hand,
and for that reason the usual tests are unreliable. Simms does
not commit himself, but in spite of the authority of Malone
and Knight he does not reject Shakspeare's authorship, but
mildly favors it: The play "exhibits a very immature condition of mind on the part of the writer. The invention,
the verse, and the philosophy, are equally humble. It was
probably the work of a youth—perhaps a boy—and that boy
might have been Shakspeare. We know nothing more utterly
absurd than this habit of testing the authorship of a work by
its intrinsic merits; applying the standards formed in the
maturer exhibitions of a great genius, to the crude and feeble
performances of his beginning."[65]

He applies the same reasoning to *Locrine*. In his customary
fashion, he quotes or summarizes the opinions of other scholars,
and laments that he does not have available any of the works
of Wentworth Smith, so that he could determine for himself
whether or not Smith wrote *Locrine* and *Titus Andronicus*.
Simms is certain that one man wrote both plays; he dissents

sharply from Knight when the English critic concludes that
the characteristics of *Locrine* are the reverse of Shakspeare
because, as Simms summarizes, the characters "speak out of
books, than because of their passions; because of the large
amount of classical and mythological imagery which *Locrine*
employs; the pedantry of the author; his frequent repetition of
phrases, in order to be rhetorical and forcible; and other like
platitudes, which need no more particular designation."[66] The
faults which led Knight to deny Shakspeare's authorship are
to Simms telling points in its favor. He holds each item to be
characteristic of a youthful author, and he is convinced that
Locrine is the work of a beginner, who still sets an exorbi-
tant value on his school classics and is more interested in
utterance than in character.

Once again Simms was writing out of his own experience.
The chief employment of the young poet was mastering the
arts of utterance, "an acquisition which must inevitably pre-
cede the knowledge of character, and the philosophy which
discriminates it happily." The faults of *Locrine* and of *Titus
Andronicus* are the same, and they are faults typical of youth:
an "excess of bloody and brutal moods; an untamed and un-
measured ferocity; a tedious sameness of tone, unsparing re-
sentments, and horrible purposes, which are left totally un-
relieved by the redeeming interposition of softer fancies—of
pity, or hope, or even love. In point of style and expression,
the resemblance of faults between the two is even more decided. . . . we have the same frequent repetition of phrases,
either to itensify the sound by reiteration, or to patch out an
imperfect line—the same free use of heathen mythology—and
the same frequent employment of fragmentary lines of Latin,
either incorporated with, or closing the paragraph. The structure of the verse of "Titus Andronicus" is singularly like that
of "Locrine." They are both full and sounding, and ample
always to overflow in the rythm. The sense is usually clear
and transparent, and the energy of the lines is quite remarkable,
showing a strength and resource in the author, in one of the
first essentials of his art, infinitely in advance of those acqui-
sitions of knowledge and thought which can only result from
constant attrition and frequent experience with the world of
man. This goes to prove the immature years of the author.
The inequalities which he exhibits are precisely such as mark

the productions of all youthful poets of genius, showing a more perfect mastery over versification than thought—showing the utterance more malleable than the idea."

As Simms noted frankly, he concurred with the German critics, especially Tieck and Schlegel, and disagreed with most of the English. He made no attempt to compare *Locrine* with *Selimus*, and disregards the possibility that the play may have been written by Peele or Greene. He believed the play to be written by Shakspeare, and that the phrase on the title page, "Newly set foorth, overseene and corrected by W. S.," meant simply that Shakspeare had slightly re-touched a play which he had written in Stratford. It is the only play that he positively attributes to Shakspeare, among the seven; he quotes at length to show that many verses have the authentic ring of the Master. The characteristics of Shakspearean verse, he decided, were manifest in "the usually abrupt manner in which the persons of the drama enter upon the business of the scene: in the noble comparisons and figures which suggest themselves, as if without effort or premeditation, to the speaker; in the presence of an overflowing and exuberant imagination; in the occasional reflection which the contemplative mood acknowledges, even in the moment of action and performance; and in that genius which frequently snatches its grace beyond the reach of art, in the felicitous expression, the happy phrase, the bold figure, the delicate and unique fancy."[67]

These are loose criteria, leaving Simms dependent on his mind and ear, and on his own training as a poet. The quotations are excellently selected to buttress the generalized characteristics that Simms has picked out as typical of Shakspeare. He makes his points clearly and well, but he is a judge who has already decided upon the verdict, and concentrates mainly on the evidence which confirms his view.

He was not willing to accept work which "shows the familiarity of a master with his tools." *The Two Noble Kinsmen* he recognized as a mature work, by one or more able craftsmen; he is willing enough to assign it to Fletcher, and to admit that the opening scene is worthy of Shakspeare. But he disagrees with Pope, Coleridge, Lamb, and the German critics and denies that Shakspeare could have had any part in it because the "versification is not his. In spite of what Mr.

Lamb has said on this subject, it lacks his flow and vivacity. The great marks of Shakspeare are his equal profundity and lucidity. He rises always with a wing from his subject, however low that may be, as we see birds skim along the surface of the ground, just above and without touching it. His most difficult thoughts, ordinarily, are those which flow musically; and the more comprehensive the range of his passion and ideas, they seem to choose for themselves an utterance of special clearness in due degree with the natural obstacles of the conception. Now, let the reader examine the metaphysical verse of the *Two Noble Kinsmen*, and he will see what embarrassments occur to the utterance of the writer in proportion to the subtlety of the sentiment."[68]

Simms felt secure in his own judgment of the play. He freely recognized its worth, but he recognized also the maturity of its authors, and he would not admit that the mature Shakspeare could have had a hand in it. He was willing to accept weak and even fumbling work from the apprentice, but not gorgeously uneven work from the master. He did not demand that all of Shakspeare's plays be of uniform excellence, based on standards determined by his finest work, but did demand a promise and a spark, and indications of youthfulness.

Since he could find none of these in *Thomas, Lord Cromwell*, he dismissed it quickly as "a very feeble effort, almost totally deficient in poetry, and lamentably wanting as a work of art."[69] *Sir John Oldcastle* presented a more serious problem, for the play had considerable merit: "The poetry is sometimes forcible and fine, if not rich and generous. It lacks the glow, the fire, the invention of Shakspeare, when on the wing, but possesses his frankness, impulse, and transparency. When Ulrici speaks of the unknown author of his play as imitating Shakspeare, or modelling himself upon him, he probably confounds two things, in their nature very different. It appears to me that, while the author of *Sir John Oldcastle* has appropriated certain of Shakspeare's materials, some two or more of his characters, and some of his incidents he has, neither in the plan of his story, nor in the structure of his verse, imitated any writer. His style of expression seems to be that of a practised writer, confident of his own mode of utterance. . . ." A bit reluctantly, since he admired the play, Simms ruled it out. He was not too much troubled by the entry in Henslowe's

Diary "to pay Mr. Monday, Mr. Drayton, Mr. Wilson, and Mr. Hathaway" for the first part, and as earnest for the second part. Simms quotes the passage, but he feels that the "very employment of no less than four hands, in the preparation of this play, would seem to declare some emergency." If four hands were required, he would be willing to concede an unlisted fifth—but he did not believe that additional collaborator, if he existed, to be Shakspeare.[70]

The Puritan belonged to an intermediate stage, and did not interest him. He was willing to follow Malone in consigning it to William Smith, or to admit it to the canon of Ben Jonson's inferior works; he mentions Dyce's identification of George Pyeboard with George Peele, purely for the reader's information; but though he noted again that maturity and strength in Shakspeare's unquestioned works were among the strongest arguments for believing in the existence of unacknowledged works, The Puritan was not among them.[71]

Simms did not pretend to himself or to his readers that he had solved any problems. His purpose in editing the works was primarily to persuade readers to share his own enthusiasm for the Elizabethan and Jacobean drama; although not averse to receiving credit for his knowledge or labor, he was at all times generously willing to lend his own prestige and popularity to the task of popularizing good but neglected work. His function as editor was first of all to make these plays accessible to readers. At the beginning of his General Introduction he stated explicitly that neither he nor the publishers proposed to decide upon the authenticity of the plays; this ticklish question would be left to "future criticism and the sagacity of the reader." He was more concerned that readers should become familiar with the merits of the plays than bogged down with problems of authorship.

In spite of this attitude, Simms perhaps inevitably devoted much of his own writing to the problem of authorship. His convictions on the subject were definite, and definitely stated. Even the greatest genius must go through a period of apprenticeship. His early works might be changelings or sons of premature birth, brought into the world before their time; they were not subject to the same tests as the "true heir" of the mature writer's labor. Yet their imperfections did not mean that they necessarily were outside the family, or that they should be consigned to oblivion. The genuine student or the youthful writer might even learn more of the processes of dramatic construction from these imperfect and sometimes obvious ,efforts than he could from something approaching perfection.

Simms objected to the criticism, best exemplified in the work of Coleridge, that could admit no weaknesses or human flaws in Shakspeare. He was quite willing to admit that in the mature work Shakspeare's artistry was equal to his genius, but not to admit that either the artistry or the genius had burst forth in full flower. His own common sense, his own experience with writers and writing, made him flatly certain that this was impossible. He realized that early work may have been lost or destroyed, but it once existed. That is the basis of his argument.

CHAPTER V

Nationalism and Sectionalism

IN AN advertisement in the first issue of the *Southern Literary Gazette*, the co-editors William Gilmore Simms and James Wright Simmons wrote that "Above all, it will be their object to encourage the efforts and do justice to the claims of native genius; and show that the natural products and flowers of our soil want but the dew and suunshine of notice, to vie in value and beauty with the more costly exotics which we import from abroad." The editors then request contributions from American writers "in general, and especially of the South," as well as from their fellow Charlestonians.[1]

An "Introduction," which certainly had Simms' approval and has earmarks of his magazine style, examined "the actual state and prospective advancement of our literature." The main if not the only hope was to emancipate it from "its present state of feudal bondage and allegiance to those 'Master Spirits' of Great Britain." One method of doing this was so to modify the language as to "form a *dialect* of our own."[2]

These were ideas that Simms was to elaborate, with many variations and degrees of violence, throughout his life. As late as November 2, 1867, he wrote in *Southern Society* that what our literature needed was the "embodied genius of RACE identified with PLACE."[3]

By that time Simms was pessimistic and disillusioned, if not hopeless. As an optimistic young man, he had felt that men of talent needed only to be awakened and given direction. In the prefatory article in the first issue of *The Cosmopolitan*, he expressed his faith that if able men could only be weaned from partisan harangues and won over "to those finer exercises of the mind," the resulting crop would be "generous and golden." He was convinced that "South Carolina is literally overflowing with talent," but it was channeled into the wrong streams, or it was dormant.[4]

There must be created an intellectual climate in which many men would write, and some of them must write a great deal. Apparently Simms believed that if a sufficient quantity of writing got done, part of it would be of high quality. Charleston lacked that climate: "You can have no idea of the general dearth of letters prevailing among us," he wrote to Lawson in 1830; "a man betraying the most remote penchant for poetry, is regarded as little less than a nuisance. Such being the temper of the time with us, you may judge of the coventry in which we labor."[5]

Except in moments of despondency, he believed the effort to create an intellectual climate that would give birth to a great literature to be worthwhile. When James Kirke Paulding was appointed Secretary of the Navy, Simms duly congratulated him, but pointedly reminded him that the "original literature of a Nation is no less important to its interests, than its valor and its virtue; and indeed, these can never be of any value, if the material of thoughts and the form of opinion, that depend so entirely upon the National writing, are derived from Foreign shores." In a country where "the tendency has been too much to ape the habits and follow the guidance of the English," it was a matter of apprehension when an able author withdrew, even temporarily, from the literary field.[6]

These privately-expressed sentiments were repeated publicly in The Magnolia, with additional material that helps to clarify what Simms meant by nationalism: "Assuming that a national literature is essential to national independence . . . to the domestic happiness of a people, and to that honorable place in the regards of strangers . . . the question naturally occurs, 'why is it that we have not this literature?' This question it must be understood, is not confined to the South. It is one equally applicable to the whole nation. America has, properly speaking, no literature of her own. The literature of a nation is of two kinds. It is that which distinguishes and illustrates, especially, the fortunes, tempers and peculiar characteristics of the people with whom it originates; or, it is that which is produced by native writers, from the common stock of human knowledge, in a fair competition with the reflective minds of other nations."[7] America had so slavishly followed British models that "All is imitative—coldly correct, and boldly imitative." But this servility was in a sense forced upon the writers by the journalistic critics with their comparative methods, so that the American work is invariably pronounced inferior to its English counterpart. What was needed, and what was lacking, was careful analysis of the individual work itself. That required thought, especially when the author uses native materials in an original manner.[8]

Critics found it easier simply to praise Bryant, Irving, Cooper, and Brockden Brown, even though they had no fame at home until they had acquired a European reputation. They had developed in spite of our neglect. Irving, in particular, had long been included among the British classics, and it "would be something of an impertinence" to claim him as an American author. The place of birth is accidental, Simms thought, and he italicized a key sentence: "*That, only, is the native soil of Genius in which it takes root and flourishes.*"[9]

Ultimately the fault is in the people. Again Simms italicizes when he argues that our lack of literature is traceable to "*the absolute and humiliating insensibility of the great body of her people to such possession.*" But men of talent gravitate into those callings which are honored and supported; in regions where the main distinction is set on money, then the writing of poetry disparages the writer in the eyes of the community. A professional Southern author who depended upon the South for support would, "*in half the number of months in the year, go without his porridge.*"[10]

At a time when many writers tried to pretend aristocratically that they did not write for money, Simms flatly declared that writing must be a profession. As editor, he encouraged his friends to write for his magazines, for this was one way to heighten and deepen the intellectual climate of the region. But he was under no delusions: "as the Literature of every nation constitutes its most enduring and most honorable monuments, it follows that permanence and premeditation must enter largely into the spirit with which the laborer sits down to his task. The works of genius are labors always; not sports. The sports of Literature may be graceful, and by possibility, great; but such can only be the case where the mind has long been drilled by habitual industry." The American sets a high value on ease and celerity of performance, forgetting or denying that the "true genius" is "one of the most toilsome and indefatigable of all human laborers."[11]

Another disadvantage of this disregard for literature was

that it forced the writer to become a dabbler in many kinds of writing, with the result that he "takes up all tasks, and botches all, or leaves them all unfinished." But the history of literature indicates that, after youthful experiments and imitations, the author does best to stick to that phase of writing for which he is best endowed by nature. Too much versatility was dangerous, and writing of various kinds proved a continued immaturity. Instead, he must "think out his own laws, and toil in obedience to the nature that works within him." Circumstances prevent the American author from addressing his "constant mind to one branch of composition." To make a living, he must publish a novel; edit, or at least contribute to, a magazine; throw off a monthly lyric; write an essay for an annual; and perhaps concoct a farce or tragedy for the stage. Here, Simms is describing the various writings of Cornelius Mathews, but he must have been fully aware that this description of diverse literary labor was even more applicable to himself and his own work. He was not optimistic that the situation would be changed, but he was certain that until "literature shall arrive at the dignity of a profession among us, our writers must continue to work under disadvantages, which will impair their confidence in themselves, lessen the strength of their conceptions, and materially diminish the force and beauty of their productions."[12]

Looking backward from the vantage-point of 1860, Simms decided that the Panic of 1837 had brought about a marked decline in the publication of novels. Before that, the novelist had been handicapped by election excitements every fourth year, and by "periodical convulsions in monetary affairs." But in 1837 society was completely unsettled. Men had no money to spend on books when they needed food, so that the novelist's "occupation, for a while, seemed gone forever, like that of Othello. . . . Few people in the business world conceive or comprehend the anxieties and degree of labor of all that class who live solely by addressing themselves, not to animal necessities, but to the popular taste." Most novelists were forced to write for cheap-paying periodicals and to tailor their work to fit editorial requirements. Book publishers introduced "the *era* of cheap literature." Instead of two well-printed volumes selling at two dollars, publishers began issuing wretched two-column pamphlets at twenty-five cents. There was no margin for paying the American author; so the British writers became "a common upon which publishers should browse at pleasure." Cheap pirated reprints flooded the market, and authorship became the least valuable element in a book's composition. Those men who could get books published were forced, in order to live, into hurried composition. Instead of an author's books getting better as he learned his craft, they became poorer as he was driven into ever hastier writing.[13]

These beliefs led Simms in the 1840s to ally himself loosely with the "Young America" group in New York led by Evert A. Duyckinck and Cornelius Mathews.[14] He liked and admired the gentle, scholarly Duyckinck. Apparently at first he liked Mathews and respected his "natural endowments," although he came increasingly to dislike him. Moreover, Simms felt that he himself had been badly treated by Lewis Gaylord Clark, editor of the *Knickerbocker*,[15] and he had "mortally offended" Charles Frederick Briggs by his sarcastic remarks on American humor, "not once suspecting him of being a professed humorist—one of your crack men in that department."[16] More important, he believed heartily in Young America's ideas for the development of a national literature, and for an international copyright. His reputation had suffered from the prejudice against a native writer, and his sales had suffered from the competition of cheaply-priced imports.

Although he hoped in each case to make some money by editing a magazine, he also regarded it as a patriotic duty to the nation and the region.[17] The first step must be "to disabuse the public mind" of the influence of English and Yankee authorities, for they have played "the devil with all that is manly and original in our literature." Even though we might be defeated, perhaps another war with Great Britain would "take us out of our leading strings."[18]

Yet this chauvinism (expressed only in a private letter to Duyckinck) must be balanced against his constant praise of English writers. One month earlier, he had recommended that Duyckinck edit a selection from the writings of Sir Samuel Egerton Brydges;[19] over many years he recommended that his nationalistic friend write an informal biography of Sir Philip Sidney, with selections that would "detach from the Arcadia all the beautiful quaint things which it contains," and giving "in full his noble defense of Poesie, one of the most symmetrical things of its kind ever written."[20] He had no desire to disparage or denigrate English authors, or to cut Americans off from their work and thought. Time and again, he advised aspiring writers to study English models such as Shakspeare, Milton, and Dryden. Even in his most patriotic and oratorical moods, it never occurred to him to suggest that his friend Bryant wrote better contemplative poetry than Wordsworth. Bryant was good, but Wordsworth clearly was better.

Rather, what infuriated Simms was the attitude of certain influential Americans who believed and wrote that "English literature is good enough for us for many hundred years to come." Although he does not put the sentence in quotation marks, he notes that "This language was actually employed by one of the American reviews of highest rank. Yet these reviews themselves are anticipated by foreign criticism, as, in most cases, they expend their analysis upon foreign publication. I have heard an American author speak with wholesale scorn of all American art, and an American painter, of superior distinction, declare that he never allowed himself to read an American book. Neither of these unfortunate persons seemed to perceive, that, in thus disparaging the native genius, they were effectually sealing their own condemnation."[21]

No group was quite as expert or as offensive in this disparagement as the editor and the main contributors to the *Knickerbocker*. Clark had become personally hostile to him, Simms thought, when he began demanding pay for his contributions to the magazine; soon after that, he pointedly omitted Simms' name from a list of "our own novelists. . . . This shows a very small nature." But Clark was full of "petty peevish vanity," and had a considerable disregard for honesty. When in 1842 the *Knickerbocker* attacked Simms' articles on Southern Literature, the editor wrote that this encouragement of sectional literature "must be regarded as a device to secure an extrinsic and undue consideration for flimsy novels." Simms felt that this and similar remarks "unjustly insinuated against my literary integrity" and proved Clark "a dirty fellow—who only avoids absolute lying from the fear of consequences. I may yet take him by the nose, and am only kept from thoroughly exposing him in print from an unwillingness to squabble with a contemporary."[22]

For all this provocation, Simms was never in his own estimation an active participant in the "War of the Literati." Duyckinck was "too gentle an enemy," for Clark was a "creature to be kicked or spit upon, not argued with or spoken to. Having given him the lie in print, and refused to know or notice him in society, it is scarcely consistent with self-esteem that I should make him a subject for remark. D. Begs me to do it." The same day he wrote to Duyckinck: "you should long ago have silenced or crushed the miserable reptile in question. Had I been living in N. Y. I could not have refrained, long ago, to have scourged him hip and thigh for the scoundrel and puppy that he is. He is of your parish not of mine . . . had you all turned in and hammered him when Poe began the game, you would have timed it rightly."[23]

In addition to feeling that the quarrel was mainly one confined to New York City, Simms was convinced that Duyckinck had erred in making Cornelius Mathews "the particular text" and main reason for his attack. Simms had welcomed contributions from his Northern friends for his magazine, and had in his own judgment leaned over backward to review their works favorably—although they considered his remarks unduly lukewarm and fault-finding. In particular, Simms had, in Miller's phrase, "gagged at Mathew's humor."[24] He had used that writer as a springboard to discuss English and American humor, or rather the notable lack of it in the Anglo-Saxon race. He thought humorous writing presented "one of the most delicate difficulties of art,—requiring a keen and quick perception, a happy susceptibility of mood, a nice regard to details, and a felicitous distribution of light and shade, with a happy mixture of pleasing but contending opposites."[25] English writers mainly lacked these qualities, for the English were not a humorous people. Essentially, their genius was for tragedy. Even Shakspeare, Scott, and Dickens employed humor mainly as a foil; underlying the "quaint and playful" surface of Charles Lamb's work is a gentle, pervasive melancholy. Since this was true of their literary ancestors, the American humorists started with a disadvantage. Moreover, our critics and publishers frequently used a wrong terminology. Mathew's *Puffer Hopkins* had been "advertised as a humorous production; and so described by half the newspaper critics in the country. A more lamentable mistake on the part of author and critic was never made."

The confusion arose partly out of calling writers like Paulding and Kennedy humorists, when they were "writers of pleasantry" instead. Even Irving, like Addison before him, was a writer of "gentlemanly pleasantries." Jack Downing was satirical, and his caricatures so closely tied to topical events that his works "are as effectually buried from sight as if they were sealed up in the catacombs of Egypt." The slick city humor of the New Yorkers died with equal quickness. The only true humor that Simms could find in this country was our rapidly-developing frontier humor—a judgment that must have offended and horrified Briggs almost as much as it did Mathews. The best work in this *genre* was to be found in Judge A. B. Longstreet's *Georgia Scenes*. Here were the finest specimens of a "rare, racy, articulate, native humor." This was original, whereas that which emanated from our seaboard cities had been "denuded of originality."[26] This naturally included the humorous work of a man who was constantly demanding originality—Cornelius Mathews.

Simms was also dubious about the demand that our poets glorify the physical aspects of the country. He agreed heartily that our scenery was diverse and beautiful enough for painter or poet, and that "the scenery of a country has always entered largely into the inspiration of the native genius." Even with her long literary history, England had produced few "merely descriptive poets . . . nor do they rank, with the single exception of Thomson, among the very noble of her train. Bloomfield was a driveller, and the rank of Somerville is low. The genius of the Anglo-Saxon would seem to be too earnest, too intensely moral in its objects, for the consideration of still life except as subordinate to the action." It is proper background, rather than a whole within itself.[27]

To be truly national, the writer need not distort his natural abilities, glorify local scenery, or even use native subjects. The fundamental distinction that he must learn is the "world-wide difference between writing *for*, and writing *from* one's people. . . . To write *from* a people is to *write* a people—to make them live—to endow them with a life and a name—to preserve them with a history forever."[28] The fact that men were writing in a democracy, with a government that left the artist of whatever kind strictly alone, seemed an encouraging symptom. Some unthinking men bemoaned the lack of literary patrons and benevolent despots, forgetting how capricious such patronage had always been. To illustrate his point, Simms characteristically turned to the region whose intellectual dominance he was attacking. For the plight of the writer under despotisms, let the reader "look to the history of Tasso for example—let him turn to that curious book of Benvenuto Cellini,—if he would see what sort of countenance is that which mere power is apt to bestow upon the labors of the man of letters or of art." Individuals with wealth and taste had done more: "Spenser owed much more to Sidney, and Shakspeare to Southampton, than either of them ever owed to Elizabeth."[29] But democracy, acting through the many rather than through one, ought to supply the support and patronage that were needed. It would do so when the proper intellectual climate had been provided.

At the same time, the writer needed certain legal safeguards that were denied to him. Some of these could be secured only through an International Copyright Law.[30] Yet Simms in his arguments advocating such a law placed the interests of the individual author as secondary to the country's "intellectual progress." Already the nation was "largely indebted" to American authors for "much of its public morality, its private virtues, its individual independence"; but we continue to be in danger of intellectual enslavement to Great Britain, especially since we speak the same language.[31] We distrust France in spite of her good will toward us because we can not speak or understand French, though we need only contrast the "thoughtful, candid, and elevated views" of travellers like Beaumont and De Tocqueville with the dishonest representations and the "cavilling and querulous peevishness" of Dickens, Marryat, and Frances Trollope to have graphic proof of the difference in attitudes.

Simms felt there were hopeful signs of a change in our point of view. For this the War of 1812, with its "humiliating disasters and exhilarating successes," was primarily responsible. When the novels of Charles Brockden Brown were published at the turn of the century, although they had "a rarely imaginative and highly original complexion," they had practically no effect upon the public taste or spirit; when, some twenty years later, Cooper's The Spy appeared, the "verdict was equally instantaneous and favorable"—a direct result of

our new spirit of independence. A national necessity had led
to the birth of a national literature.[32]

That literature had failed to develop fully because we had
failed to develop a profession of letters. Simms roundly declared that "Nothing has ever come from amateur performances in letters or the arts." There must be habitual daily
labor and the practice of exercises intended to lead to perfection. Again he turned to England for his illustration: "How
little we owe to the Sackvilles, the Rochesters, the Carews,
the Sucklings . . . the tribe of clever gentlemen about town,
—and how much we owe to the day-laborers in letters." In
the first rank of these constant workers he included Shakspeare, Ben Jonson, Samuel Johnson, Pope, and Dryden: men
who left behind them "a vast storehouse of material, wild
song and wondrous story, from which the more slenderly
endowed moderns will long continue to replenish their ex-
hausted senses." These men and the galaxy of Elizabethan
dramatists had in the main lived by literature, sometimes "in
spite of degradation, poverty, public scorn and private misery."
They were professional writers, not amateurs. In America
also it was necessary that authors be able to live by their profession, if they were to develop their natural abilities. Even so,
they sacrificed enough, for "Literature is a self-denying vocation, tasking thought, and imagination, and sensibility, vex-
ing the dreams—depriving the nights of renovating rests, enfeebling the frame and souring the temper."[33] There were
men willing to sacrifice themselves. But financially the position
of the American author had grown worse instead of better.

Drawing heavily for his facts on a pamphlet by George
Palmer Putnam, Simms presented evidence that many American
books were annually being published in London, sometimes
slightly doctored up (titles altered, prefaces suppressed, even
in a few instances substituting names of English cities) so that
they would appear to be English books. Rarely did an
American author receive any royalty from these publications.

At home, the picture was even darker. In 1834, American
publishers had brought out nineteen volumes of original
novels and tales, as compared with ninety-five reprints—a
degree of competition that was ruinous to writers of fiction.
Usually for these reprints the publisher paid nothing to the
British author and he ruthlessly sacrificed the quality of com-

position, paper, and binding, with the result that many of these books could be bought in New York for one-fifth what they cost in London. Taking advantage of the cheaper postal rates for newsprint, they issued many pirated works in folio format and distributed them at a fraction of the cost of books and magazines.[34]

Unscrupulous publishers took every advantage of law, and of the lack of law. Reputable publishers were the creatures of the system. But the author was the victim. Since only in the regular employment of authors could a good native literature be produced, this meant that eventually the intellectual life of the country would decline. Simms was concerned for himself and for other individual authors, but his main argument was that only through international copyright protection could we develop a profession of letters. This he regarded as essential to the development of a valid and vigorous American literature.

II

By 1850 Simms was even prepared to welcome England as an ally in the struggle of the South with the North. He was prepared for the dissolution of the Union, and thought it would come within five years.[35] He lashed out angrily at "Yankee historians" who vilified the South not only about the present controversy but even falsified the record of the South's part in the Revolutionary War.[36] Although he continued to visit New York frequently and to publish there, he recommended that Southerners patronize their own rather than the Northern watering places and resorts so as to avoid "subservience to northern opinion."[37] The nationalist was rapidly becoming submerged in the sectionalist.

This was a gradual development. The prospectus of the *Southern Literary Gazette* in 1828 had made the point that a healthy regional literature was needed in order that there might be a healthy national literature. His reasoned belief on this is clearly and precisely stated in the dedicatory letter to *The Wigwam and the Cabin*, dated September 20, 1856, well after he had become a secessionist: "One word for the material of these legends. It is local, sectional—and to be *national* in literature, one must needs be *sectional*. No one mind can fully or fairly illustrate the characteristics of any great country; and he who shall depict *one section* faithfully, has made his proper and sufficient contribution to the great work of *national* illustration. I can answer for it, confidently, that these legends represent, in large degree, the border history of the south. . . . I need not apologize for the endeavor to cast over the actual that atmosphere from the realms of the ideal, which, while it constitutes the very element of fiction, is neither inconsistent with intellectual truthfulness, nor unfriendly to the great policies of human society."[38]

In 1828 he had been a Unionist opposed to Nullification. Using round figures, Simms wrote to the political-minded James Henry Hammond in 1847 that "I should have arrived at my [present] conclusions without your aid, if I had not, after my repudiation 20 years ago as a Union man, dismissed as much as possible from my mind the consideration of subjects over which it appeared to me I was destined to have no control." Yet both the earlier and the later position seemed logical enough: although a believer in states' rights, he did not believe that a state which remained within the Union had the right to nullify federal laws. On the other hand, it did have the right to withdraw or secede whenever it wished to do so.[39]

However confident he may have been that the South could be politically independent, Simms had little confidence that it could be intellectually independent. Possibly his long experience in one field and relative inexperience in the other adequately explains this. He summed up his own experiences in a pessimistic letter to the editor of the *Magnolia*: "I have had so much experience, either as an editor or as a contributor, in the making of Southern Magazines, and know so thoroughly their history, and the inevitable event, that my conviction of the almost certain fate which awaits them, inspires me with a feeling, very like disgust, when I am told of any new experiment of this kind in contemplation. I know, and can predict, the usual story of confident hope and bold assurance with which they commonly begin. The editor feels his strength and his friends promise theirs. His neighbors pledge their subscriptions, and the beginning of the work is made with considerable energy and eclat.

"But the progress of a few months soon undeceives the confiding, and blunts the energy even of the most sanguine. The editor discovers that he has overtasked himself. His contributors—men, generally, in our country, devoted to other professions—can only write for him at moments of leisure, which good nature and an amicable desire to oblige, prompts them to employ in this manner. He is necessarily compelled to wait upon them for their articles, which, good, bad, or indifferent, he is compelled to publish. The constant drain upon himself, enfeebles his imagination and exhausts his intellect. He has little time for thought, and no opportunity for the exercise of taste and fancy; and the station which he has self-assumed, so far from being a chair of state, from which he may dispense judgment, and exercise a dignified authority over the world of letters, becomes one of pain, disquiet, and the most unintermitted mental drudgery. . . . The printer, who seldom is a capitalist, clamors for his monthly dues, and the subscriber recedes from the subscription list, the moment that he is called upon for his." The magazine as a rule is wretchedly printed on cheap paper, and the innocuous material is honeycombed with errors. The inevitable result is the "early abandonment of an attempt in which nothing has been realized but discredit, annoyance, and expense."[40]

Yet the contributor fared little better than the editor. If an amateur, he was forced to expend a disaproportionate amount of time and energy on an unfamiliar task. Even then, his work is not likely to be good, for the "*habit of literary composition is an essential element to all successful periodical writing.*" If a professional, he knows ahead of time that he is largely wasting his labors. Here too Simms could speak with personal authority: "When I sit down to write for a Southern periodical—which I do only as a professional duty—I do so under the enfeebling conviction that my labors and those of the editor are taken in vain;—that the work will be little read, seldom paid for, and will finally, and after no very long period of spasmodic struggle, sink into that gloomy receptacle of the 'lost and abused things of earth,' which, I suspect, by this time possesses its very sufficient share of Southern periodical literature."[41]

Yet he was continually being tempted to edit Southern magazines, and he frequently yielded to temptation. Before the death of *The Magnolia* he had agreed (October 1843) to help with the *Southern Quarterly Review*: "My motive," he wrote to B. F. Perry, "is simply that we may have at least one organ among ourselves to which we may turn when it becomes necessary to express Southern feelings and opinions."[42] He recognized that some of "our institutions are peculiar" and required a vigorous defense which would not be welcomed or published by editors outside the region: "as a Southron I am anxious to maintain among us a high organ of opinion, as well in literature, as in politics; at once for the preservation of our rights and institutions, and for the assertion of our domestic mind."[43] More than most sections, the South needed a periodical literature: "The very sparseness of our population, which renders it so difficult a matter to sustain the Periodical, is the very fact that renders its existence and maintenance so necessary." With few cities, with books expensive and difficult to procure, with relatively little "attrition and collision" of minds, the South was unusually dependent on oratory and on magazines for the intellectual stimulation of its adult people.[44]

The planter who could afford it should take "one or more British and French periodicals, and one from each great city in the Union." True, the reflective reader would find these foreign works in general to be better edited and more thoughtfully written than local ones. But the planter should take these also, partly to stimulate his own mental activity and parly to stimulate that of writers within the region. The South could not hope to compete with Europe in "those respects of literature which involve absolute possessions of learning and art. . . . It is in the exhibition of *native* and *original* endowments alone, that American Literature can ever acquire or deserve reputation." The Southern magazine, viewed in this light, not only afforded the fledgling author an opportunity to publish; it also encouraged the older one, for there "is no greater stimulus to literary effort, than to feel that your neighbors appreciate your toils, and are proud of them." Many magazines had failed, and more would fail, but if they had disseminated thought and stimulated mental activity, "who shall venture to say that this failure was complete?"[45]

In the 1850s he believed that there was a promising intellectual ferment in the South, and he did all that he could to encourage young writers like Henry Timrod, Paul Hamilton Hayne, and John Esten Cooke. Reviewing the poetry of the very minor Howard Caldwell, Simms recommended a generous patronage of Southern authors without too much regard to literary quality, for only by encouraging many young authors could the region develop a few good ones.[46] Already the quality of the literary work showed marked improvement. But the South must struggle against many handicaps. It had no large city, to serve as a commercial and intellectual center; no publishing houses, but only printers who occasionally issued books without having the facilities to distribute them; the educational system was newly-established and inadequate. Of the four essential sources of a prosperous, vigorous society—agriculture, commerce, manufacture, and education—the South had fully developed and used only the first, and no "*purely* agricultural people, anywhere, has ever produced a national literature."[47]

But his mind had become increasingly engrossed with political and (after 1861) with military problems. When asked for contributions by the *Southern Illustrated News*, he defended his literary inactivity: "At this time, it is not easy to do anything of length, involving much elaborate design. . . . To do justice to the public, or to one's self, in letters, implies a perfectly calm mind, much leisure, and freedom from distracting occupations. Your whole mind must be concentrated on your subject. But who can give his whole mind to, or concentrate his thoughts upon abstract topics, when the whole country is heaving with the throes of a mighty revolution. . . . We are now *living* the first grand epic of our newly-born Confederacy. We are *making* the materials for the drama, and for future songs and fiction; and, engaged in the actual event, we are in no mood for delineating its details, or framing it to proper laws of art, in any province. This must be left to other generations, which, in the enjoyment of that peace and independence for which we are now doing battle, will be able to command the leisure for those noble and generous arts by which nations best assert their claims to independence, and secure a proud immortality."[48]

After the war, he went back to his belief that good sectionalism was an essential part of good nationalism. On the surface, this might not seem to be true. He confessed that his *War Poetry of the South* was "sectional in its character, and indicative of a temper and a feeling which were in conflict with nationality; yet, now that the States of the Union have been resolved into one nation, this collection is essentially . . . the property of the whole." Simms intended that the book should do honor to the South, but he insisted that it "belongs to the national literature, and will hereafter be regarded as constituting a proper part of it."[49]

III

For all his vehement advocacy of a native literature, Simms was never in any sense an intellectual isolationist. As a young man he attempted to remedy what he considered defects in his education; in addition to reading omnivorously and exhausting the libraries of his friends, "I picked up a little Latin, French, Spanish, Italian, and even German enough to enable me to dabble in translations, of which I have made a good many."[50] As a very young editor, he thought that the overweening British influence might be counteracted, and the weaknesses of British thought exposed, by a knowledge of European writers: "When we shall have cultivated a more intimate acquaintance with the literature of France, Spain, Germany, and Italy, we shall then at length have discovered that for the last quarter of a century, we have indeed been following blind guides."[51] Years later, in his papers on a copyright law, Simms noted that one way to emancipate us from intellectual enslavement to England was to encourage the reading of European works, especially German.[52] Much later, he recommended to his young friend Mary Lawson that in addition to reading widely in English she should "acquire the continental languages, Italian and Spanish. Why not the German. Half a dozen young Ladies might get up an evening class, three times a week, at their several houses, and under a good tutor, would in one summer learn to read freely either of the two former; perhaps speak them; and in one year would surely go pretty deep in a knowledge of the German. But for my labours, and my incessant practice of English, I should be a good German, French, Spanish and Ital. scholar. Alas for me, I have now pretty much forgotten all that I ever knew; for, where the language is not one daily spoken in our ears, it must be daily made familiar to our eyes."[53]

Undoubtedly he read foreign books mainly in translation. Many of these books he reviewed, sometimes glancingly in such a comment as "Balzac is one of the best of their modern tale writers," in noticing *Father Goriot*;[54] sometimes dogmatically, as when he asserted of *The Works of Montaigne* that "We do not err a jot when we say to our readers that this collection of Montaigne is quite as important to an English library as the essays of Johnson, Goldsmith and Addison."[55] He recommended the historian and biographer Lamartine as "a delightful companion, though to be distrusted as a teacher."[56] But he also warned his readers that it was difficult to find satisfactory translations of most French works, and almost impossible in the case of Victor Hugo, with his forcible and original but often paradoxical philosophical thoughts, his poetic fancy, and his gorgeous imagery.[57]

It seems probable that Simms' great interest in German literature was aroused, certainly stimulated, by Thomas Carlyle. In reviewing a four-volume collection of *The Miscellanies*, Simms wrote that "Here is a vast body of literature, of that valuable sort, at once historical and suggestive, which makes the reader to know, and compels him to think. . . . They cover German literary history more completely, we think, than has ever been done by any or all of the writers who have attempted it." Through reading and translating German, Carlyle "gradually began to think in German, and as gradually began to depart from English simplicity in diction . . . he sought to produce verbal and dramatic effects in narrative, historical, and philosophical composition," largely through adapting the pattern and structure of the German language to English. He had ideally fitted himself to deal with German thought as expressed in its philosophy and literature.[58]

J. Wesley Thomas has presented convincing arguments that German writers greatly influenced Simms' own writings: "Germany's contributions to Simms' short stories consisted primarily of supernatural occurrences, exotic settings, and an irrational atmosphere. Germany influenced Simms' early novels, on the other hand, by providing him with definite psychological problems and the technique for their expositions."[59] There was a third, although less direct, influence, which Simms noted in an early critical article: "At present there is, perhaps, no portion of Literary history of more importance to us, than that of Germany. Rising as we are into a state of refined Literature, and about to establish for ourselves a national character, it must be advantageous to examine those principles by the adoption of which her people have risen up to an independence of thought, and have become eminent in the several departments of learning."[60]

Of the German authors, Goethe seemed to him easily the most important, for "Goethe was emphatically the great artist of the age."[61] Apparently he read *Faust* in the original and in translation; he made at least four translations from Goethe's poem, using one as a key headnote to *Confession*. But the clearest borrowing, or at least parallelism, is to be found in *The Cassique of Kiawah*: Colonel Berkeley's activities in draining the Carolina swamps, reclaiming good land from the marsh and the forests, constructing houses, and working for a better way of life for other human beings seem clearly intended to recall to the minds of knowledgeable readers the second part of *Faust*.[62]

Schiller also could be a wholesome influence. Cornelius Mathews had gone back to pre-historic times in America in *Behemoth*, but he had attempted to tell the story in prose. If Mathews had studied the art of narrative as Schiller had, he would have known better: the German poet "would not have hesitated a single instant as to the necessity of treating it in a purely poetical manner. He would have felt the dangers and difficulties in the way of a prose narrative, which, whatever may be the character of the style employed, or the proem of the author, necessarily promises a greater soberness of fancy, and a sterner grasp upon the reins of imagination, than is necessary where the story is told in verse."[63] Schiller also had left behind a rich store of material from which Simms borrowed freely: Mr. Thomas is especially convincing in pointing out similarities in ideas and characterization between Schiller's novelette *Der Verbrecher* and *Confession*, and between the play *Die Rauber* and the novel *The Kinsmen*.[64]

Some of his more bizarre and Gothic tales (notably the Faustian "Carl Werner" and "Comrade Weickhoff") Simms set in Germany, on the ground that it was a land "renowned for its superstitions, its wild fancies, its marvelous imaginations. The minds of its people have become spiritualized by the popular faith; and thought takes the shape of poetry at its birth, and fancy is busy everywhere."[65] This Germany of his imagination was largely created in his mind out of the writings not only of Goethe and Schiller but also from those of Jean Paul Frederick Richter ("one of the most capricious, fantastic, and playful of the modern writers");[66] Gottfried August Bürger ("the wild and mystical author of *Lenore*"); [67] Baron de la Motte Fouqué (*Undine und Sintram* are "among the very best specimens of that fanciful and sublimated style of conception and composition, which, in latter days, we have learned to associate almost too exclusively with the genius of the German");[68] and E. T. A. Hoffman, Joseph von Eichendorff, and even the Baron Münchausen tall tales provided grist for his own literary mill.[69]

Although as editor Simms frequently requested articles on French and Spanish literature and published many translations, he was even more interested in those parts of their histories which had become a part of American history. Precisely because so little factual material was available, the "frequent and unsuccessful attempts at colonization" by the English, French, and Spanish offered an ideal opportunity for the novelist, dramatist, or poet. The artist would need to read widely in collateral histories and to study the events of the period closely, not as sources of facts, but as a way toward understanding "the moral and social characteristics of the several nations engaged in these discoveries." With this understanding, the writer would do no violence to history: "It is by the excellence of the art that the fiction is converted into truth; and all malleable conjecture, not conflicting with the unquestionable and the known, is truth sufficient for all the purposes of poetry."[70]

The French colonial material he utilized in a semi-history, semi-romance, *The Lily and the Totem*, that dealt with the Huguenot colony in Florida. He had been careful to make "the fiction simply tributary, and always subordinate to the fact. . . . My labor has not been to make, but to perfect, a history; not to invent facts, but to trace them out to seemingly inevitable results;—to take the premise and work out the problem;—recognize the meagre record which affords simply a general outline;—and endeavor, by a severe induction, to supply its details and processes." He had, he felt, been able "to supply, from the *probable*, the apparent deficiencies of the actual."[71]

Spain and Spanish-America interested him even more, possibly because that influence had been much nearer the Southern colonies in time and in place.[72] Spaniards had in fact played an important and conquering role in *The Lily and the Totem*. But much earlier, as a boy of seventeen, he had written a play about Roderick the Goth and the Saracenic invasion of Spain; he had read Spanish literature with considerable enthusiasm; in 1838, remembering his "almost forgotten tragedy," he "converted the story into prose": *Pelayo* and its sequel, *Count Julian*.[73] Moreover, he had personally seen in Mississippi a rude cross that he believed marked the grave of one of DeSoto's followers.[74] DeSoto and his fellow-explorers were almost ideal protagonists. Part of the story of Balboa he used in *The Damsel of Darien*, and made him the hero of a longish poem, "Vasco Nunez";[75] Ponce de Leon, endowed with a good many Byronic or Don Juan qualities, is a main character in the uncompleted poem "Donna Florida"; DeSoto himself plays a major part in *Vasconselos*. This last is Simms' most ambitious work on a Spanish or Spanish-Indian subject, and the material seemed to him ideal: "As a drama embodying a most curious and interesting progress, during a singularly-attractive period in our ante-colonial history, the invasion (not the conquest—very far from it!) of the empire of the Floridian (Appalachian) savage, by Hernan de Soto, affords a vast and fertile field for him who works in the provinces of art in fiction."[76]

Spanish characters and the threat of invasion to the English colonies add contrast and tension to several tales and novels. This is especially true of *The Cassique of Kiawah*, for the heroine is Spanish, and the Spanish attack on Port Royal is described. Here too are good examples of Simms' translations of Spanish songs and ballads.[77]

Simms was ready enough to admit influences and parallelisms when he remembered them. Probably he was unconscious of many of his borrowings. When aware of them, he undoubtedly felt that he had made the material, the technique, the history, or the character entirely his own. For the artist was at once individual and eclectic, and each man must work in his own way: "The subject must suggest its own modes of treatment to him who conceives it. What would strike one mind as singularly suitable for the uses of the artist, would scarcely commend itself to the peculiar genius of another." For that reason, the artist must be left entirely free to write of American or of foreign subjects, even though Simms stressed the advantages of writing about the known and the familiar. But the writer could not write out of a vacuum: "When our people shall really have acquired some intellectual appetites in sufficient number to make and mould the popular taste; and books shall have become an aliment as absolutely necessary to us as brandy and tobacco—we shall then have the poet and the song."[78]

CHAPTER *VI*

A Summing Up

I HOPE that this survey of William Gilmore Simms' work as literary critic has indicated clearly that he was a good but not a great critic. He wrote vigorously and provocatively, basing his ideas and judgments on what he regarded as sound common sense. Unfortunately, he wrote hurriedly, and allowed himself little or no time for revision. One result was that, like Edgar Allan Poe, he mainly hammered out his critical principles in reviews, or in articles in which the review of a book or books served as a springboard. Frequently these article-reviews present admirably his general principles; sometimes they are perfunctory, and heavily padded with quotations. Unlike Poe, he showed little interest in developing and refining a rounded aesthetic that would justify a particular kind of literature (in Poe's case, a literature suitable for magazines). Only in his effort to justify the romance, as contrasted with the novel, did Simms attempt to construct something approaching an aesthetic. Perhaps for this reason, the Preface to *The Yemassee* remains his most influential critical work.[1]

As a critic, he tried always to be genial but just. He warned his friend James Lawson "not to suffer yourself to be deceived with a dogma . . . which teaches a doctrine so unjust as to make fault finding the merit of a Critic. The merit of a Critic, like the merit of any other judge whether elected or self constituted is to see that justice is done,—not to desire to pass judgment, but to award justice. . . . In reviewing a work, you are required not merely to review the story,—if that were all that were required from the critic, there would not be a butcher's boy who could not form as good and correct an opinion as the wisest scholar; but you are to review the thousand qualities of the writer—his skill as an artist, his moral sense, his taste, his knowledge of character, of human passion, and foibles, his powers of expression, and the range and the degree of enthusiasm which is possessed by his genius. To do this effectually calls for long study of these qualities, an intimate knowledge of the writings which are similar, and corresponding sympathies with a kind of performance to which they belong. A heart susceptible of human feelings, and a mind not rendered obtuse by a particular and foreign direction in its pursuits, are also necessary to so serious a task."[2] In a concise and well-phrased definition, Simms perhaps unfortunately put one other duty upon the critic: "Neither to praise nor to blame is the object of true criticism. Justly to discriminate, firmly to establish, wisely to prescribe and honestly to award—these are the true aims and criteria of criticism."[3]

Within his limits, Simms attempted to embody these critical precepts in his own reviews. He made a manful and usually successful effort to be objective in his judgments. He was generously indignant about the niggardly recognition given to James Fenimore Cooper; he disliked intensely that type of comparative criticism which was interested only in elevating one author at the expense of another, and pleaded instead for an analytic and intrinsic criticism. His fear of English intellectual domination did not cloud his estimates of English authors, past or contemporary; his desire for a national literature did not lead him, in his own judgment, to minimize the faults of American authors; his intense sectionalism did not blind him to the merits as well as the faults of the New England writers. Simms had his full share of convictions and prejudices, and he acted on them: he dissected *Uncle Tom's Cabin* with more wrath than dispassion, yet he freely admitted that Mrs. Stowe wrote with power and passion. Many of his analyses and judgments seem today well-founded and just; his over-praise of a novelist like Bulwer is readily understandable on the ground of a contemporary appeal that has largely vanished with the years. In his literary judgments he attempted always to be honest with himself and with his readers.

His critical theories often seem better than his fictional and poetic practices. Largely because of his habit of hasty writing and his dislike of revision, he frequently violated his

own concepts of unity and of design, especially in the romance. It was easier to digress, to invent on the spur of the
moment, and to discourse on historical matters, than it was
to make or to follow a severe, carefully-planned, and artistic
design.

At times he seems to ante-date Henry James in his comments on morality in art, but there is at once a curious kinship
and a curious dissimilarity: when Simms declares that a writer
is moral only in proportion to his truthfulness, he puts the
primary emphasis on the writer's truthfulness to life, whereas James emphasizes truth in the writer's art. Clearly, Simms'
ideas left much freer room for the handling of story and
characters, but this freeness undoubtedly worked to his disadvantage. It is not that he was unconcerned with the problems of art; as his criticism reveals, he was concerned with
these problems, but he did not set a primary value on them.
Genius, inspiration, bold and original thought could more than
counterbalance any defects in strict artistry. Yet he was
troubled by these blemishes in his own works, and sometimes
apologized for them. But he also felt that, for one of his
own ardent temperament, his way of writing was best.
This was rationalization, but it may also have been true.

It is unfortunate although perhaps inevitable that the one
collection of his critical articles was "devoted entirely to
American topics."[4] The articles for *Views and Reviews* were
selected and the two volumes published in the 1840s, when
Simms was most highly involved in the Nationalism controversy; the work was planned for a series called the "Library
of American Books," under the general editorship of Evert
A. Duyckinck, a prime mover in the "Young America" group.
This gives the book a certain unity, but at the expense of a
fair presentation of Simms' critical views. There is no reason
to doubt that he believed everything he said here. But his
anti-English feelings are not properly compensated for by
his sane and appreciative comments on English writers and
writing; his patriotic fervor is not balanced by his admiration
for foreign, especially German, authors. It is not that the
individual judgments in this collection give a warped or
distorted impression. Yet the totality does. Simms was neither
as narrowly nor as ignorantly prejudiced as a casual reading
of *Views and Reviews* has led some literary historians to infer.

He believed that it was one function of American critics and criticism to encourage the development of a healthy native literature, but an equally valid function was to bring about a healthy intellectual climate. Such a climate would inevitably result in a healthy native literature. But it could not be established in or by ignorance. The intellectual climate he envisioned must be based on international knowledge and cosmopolitan appreciation. As a result, many of his newspaper commentaries were designed simply to "apprize" his readers of what was going on in the literary world. He did not believe this without value: when the people demanded a first-rate literature, writers would appear who would be capable of producing great poems, dramas, and novels. His better articles go beyond this. Through them also, undoubtedly, he hoped to teach his readers discrimination and judgment, but he realized that the only way to demonstrate that was by clearly stating his principles and by making just discriminations and wise judgments in his own criticism.

Notes

Chapter I NOTES: SIMMS SELF-REVEALED

[1]*The Letters of William Gilmore Simms.* Collected and Edited by Mary C. Simms Oliphant, Alfred Taylor Odell, and T. C. Duncan Eaves. With an Introduction by Donald Davidson and a Biographical Sketch by Alexander S. Salley. Five Volumes. Columbia: The University of South Carolina Press, 1952-56. The editors of the *Letters* have done a painstaking, admirable job. The location of every known letter is given, and many letters have been newly and correctly re-dated after a careful study of the internal evidence. Letters that have come to light since the work started (including valuable ones to Bryant, Cooper, and Kennedy) are included in an appendix to the fifth volume. The footnotes are invaluable for a study of Simms' life and especially of his work: quotations are identified; personal and historical circumstances are adequately explained; whenever possible, the anonymous contributors to magazines that Simms edited have been listed, along with the titles of their works; the number of Simms' identifiable pseudonyms (now approximately fifty) has been greatly increased; generous illustrative quotations have been given from Simms' own writings, from reviews of his published books, and from letters written to him. The editorial paraphernalia is elaborate, but practically all of it is useful.

[2]Jay B. Hubbell, *The South in American Literature,* 572. Hubbell's treatment of Simms is excellent. John Esten Cooke's phrase is quoted in Hubbell, 576.

[3]Vernon L. Parrington, *Main Currents in American Thought,* II, 127. Although not entirely reliable, Parrington is enthusiastic and in general sound in his discussion. Parrington assumes that he had "no Latin or Greek" (125). Although his knowledge of Greek literature seems to have been derived from translation, he knew Latin; characteristically, in an agricultural oration, he drew heavily on Virgil's *Georgics.* See "Ancient and Modern Culture: Extracts from an Agricultural Oration," *Magnolia,* IV (May, 1842), 308-11.

[4]*Letters,* V, 383.

[5]James Henry Hammond wrote Simms a generally complimentary letter about this October 1849 issue, but complained humorously, "by the Lord, if you touch off 54 subjects every quarter, what will you leave for your correspondents?" Quoted in *Letters,* II, 538n.

[6]Quoted in *Letters,* III, 193-94n.

[7]*Letters,* I, 400.

[8]*Letters,* III, 173. Simms frequently complained that it was more fatiguing not to write than it was to write.

[9]Quoted in *Letters*, III, 15n.

[10]See especially his letters to Paul Hamilton Hayne, *Letters*, IV, 437-38, and to John R. Thompson, 438-39.

[11]For a fairly full report on the lectures and their reception, see *Letters*, III, 454-69.

[12]*Letters*, IV, 265.

[13]*Letters*, IV, 368.

[14]*Letters*, IV, 315.

[15]*Letters*, IV, 318.

[16]*Letters*, IV, 436.

[17]*Letters*, IV, 601.

[18]*The Wigwam and the Cabin*, 4.

Chapter II   NOTES: ON NOVELS AND NOVELISTS

[1]C. Hugh Holman, "The Status of Simms," in *American Quarterly*, X (July, 1958), 181-85. Quotation on p. 183.

[2]*Letters*, I, 271. He wrote to James Henry Hammond in 1847 that "my income from Literature which in 1835 was $6000 per annum, is scarce $1500 now, owing to the operation of cheap reprints which pay publishers and printers profits only and yield the author little or nothing."

[3]*Letters*, V. 409, for this and following quotation. See also Bradsher, *Mathew Carey*, 96. Simms' *History of South Carolina* continued to be used for several decades.

[4]*Letters*, V, 409.

[5]*Letters*, III, 388.

[6]This and the immediately following quotations are taken from Alexander Cowie's edition of *The Yemassee* (New York, 1937), pp. 3-7.

[7]*Letters*, III, 412.

[8]Simms, "The Writings of James Fenimore Cooper," in *Views and Reviews*, 210-11. First published in *The Magnolia*, NS I (Sept., 1842), 129-39. Simms' belief in inspiration as a major factor in artistic creativity was stated frequently. He believed that an author "may create, but he cannot control. It is upon this very condition that he is permitted to create. The Being, once filled with the breath of life, and having made his appearance on the stage of human action, must thenceforward conform to necessities over which the author exercises no authority" (*Vasconselos*, 366). Simms frequently praised domestic novels, however. He found Mrs. Gaskell's *Cranford* particularly refreshing because the characters reminded him of certain Charlestonians "who really believe that we are favored above all the sons of the earth, and occupy in fact the original site of the Garden of Eden" (*SQR*, NS IX [Jan., 1854], 245).

[9]Introduction, *The Partisan*, VII. In a plea for the supernatural (*The Wigwam and the Cabin*, 2-3), Simms wrote: "Our story-tellers are so resolute to deal in the real, the actual only, that they venture on no subjects the details of which are not equally vulgar and susceptible of proof. . . . I very much doubt whether the poet, the painter, the sculptor, or the romancer, ever yet lived, who had not some strong bias—a leaning, at least,—to a belief in the wonders of the invisible world. Certainly, the higher orders of poets and painters, those who create and invent, must have a strong taint of the superstitious in their composition."

[10]*Letters*, I, 54. In *The Golden Christmas*, 154, Simms places a higher value on characterization than his own fictional practice might seem to warrant: "The artist does not make events; they make themselves. They

belong to the characterization. The author makes the character. If this be made to act consistently,—and this is the great necessity in all works of fiction—events flow from its action necessarily, and one naturally evolves another, till the whole action is complete. Here is the whole secret of the novelist." In "Modern Prose Fiction" (SQR, XV, 44; April, 1849) he notes: "To seem like truth was, still, as it has ever been, in every age, the object of fiction."

[11]Confession, 8-9.

[12]See, for example, Richard Hurdis, 10, and especially Mellichampe, 6: In defending bringing "the vulgar and the vicious mind" into the story, Simms declares that "I am persuaded that vulgarity and crime must always preponderate—dreadfully preponderate—in the great majority during a period of war."

[13]Letters, I, 67. In his appreciative essay, "Weems, the Biographer and Historian" (Views and Reviews, II, 137), he noted that Weems exercised the "privilege of the old Historians" in "putting speeches into the mouths of his heroes . . . this deceived nobody. The deception was a very innocent one; for, it so happened, that his parties, thus furnished with speech, invariably talked like Weems himself."

[14]Mellichampe, 2, for this and following quotation.

[15]Katharine Walton, 474.

[16]Mellichampe, 3. Simms has a parenthetical reference to the true story in Katharine Walton, 279. The two following quotations are from Katharine Walton, 295n and 329n.

[17]Richard Hurdis, 401n. In the Advertisement, 10-11, Simms emphasizes the fact that he had written out of direct personal knowledge: "I knew Stuart, the captor of Murrell, personally . . . some of my scenes, and several of my persons were sketched from personal observation . . . the facts here employed are beyond question." In the Dedication to The Wigwam and the Cabin he similarly asserts (pp. 4-5): "I have seen the life—have lived it—and much of my material is the result of a very early personal experience."

[18]SQR, XXIV (July, 1853), 218. For a full account of Simms' handling of Uncle Tom's Cabin, see S.P.C. Duvall, "W. G. Simms's Review of Mrs. Stowe," American Literature, 30 (March, 1958), 107-17.

[19]SQR, XXIV, 217. Simms frequently described his own novels as dramas. In a notice of Love Me Little, Love Me Long ("Literary Docket," Charleston Mercury, June 21, 1859), Simms thought Charles Reade had borrowed "too many of his tastes and habits from the stage. The modern novel is, in truth, dramatic in its character, and has thus done more than anything besides to unseat the drama in the popular affection."

[20]See Eutaw, 116, 117.

[21]Richard Hurdis, 11-12. See also p. 72: "Let me unfold the doings of others, necessarily connected with my own, which are proper to be made known to the reader in this place, though only known to me long after their occurrence."

[22]For one example, see Eutaw, 339-40.

[23]Letters, I, 63. This lack of personal familiarity might also be a psychological handicap. In a "Lorris" Letter, Charleston Mercury, Dec. 29, 1859, he thought G. P. R. James' Ticonderoga not among his "happiest efforts," for in his first attempt to employ American materials, James "seems to have lacked confidence in his American resources." Similarly, when Cooper turned to Europe for literary material, he by no means failed but the stories were "inferior in interest—there was less felicitous display of scenery, and, as the author was less confident of his knowledge, much of the

description was vague, and the characters, framed under hurried glimpses and imperfect observation, were necessarily formal and frigid, wanting in earnestness and life, slow in action, and feeble in will and purpose" (*Views and Reviews*, I, 225). In the Preface (vi) to *Count Julian*, Simms indicated that he might have erred ("with the view of obtaining novelty in my material") in trying to deal with the unfamiliar: "An author, to whom the *locale* of his action is so very important (as it is with me) to the spirit of his narrative, is perhaps always more happy in his achievements when he looks at home." See also his comments to J. P. Kennedy, *Letters*, II, 159-60.

[24]*Views and Reviews*, I, 42-43. In explaining what he had attempted to do in his semi-fictional treatment of the Huguenots in Florida, Simms noted that "It is by raising the tone of the history, warming it with the hues of fancy, and making it dramatic by the continued exercise of art, rather than by any actual violation of its recorded facts, that I have endeavored to awaken interest." He had attempted "to supply, from the *probable*, the *apparent* deficiencies of the *actual*" (*The Lily and the Totem*, v).

[25]*Views and Reviews*, I, 23-25. See also *Letters*, V, 399-400. Re-surveying the subject in two articles, "American Resources in Fiction" (*Southern Society*, Nov. 9, 1867 and Dec. 7, 1867), Simms notes that various phases of early American history are becoming more suitable for art as the details fade with time. But we are too impatient, forgetting that it took a thousand years of national growth to produce a Shakspeare. The true builder or creator will appear in time: "the true Prospero, with his rod of divination, will drive Caliban to his cave, and release Ariel from his oak."

[26]*SQR.*, XVII (July, 1850), 318.

[27]*Vasconselos*, 1.

[28]*Letters*, II, 264-65. He objected particularly to such scientific historians as Barthold Niebuhr: "It is not our purpose to disparage the learned ingenuity, the keen and vigilant judgment, the great industry, the vast erudition and sleepless research of this coldly inquisitive man;—yet, what a wreck has he made of the imposing structure of ancient history, as it comes to us from the hands of ancient art. . . . We prefer one Livy to a cloud of such witnesses as M. Niebuhr" (*Views and Reviews*, I, 23n).

[29]*Letters*, IV, 181. In a discussion of Byron's work, however, he noted that a man writes best about "one's self, one's country, and one's religion," for then he writes out of "the fulness of his own soul" (*Views and Reviews*, I, 38-39). See also *Count Julian*, vi-vii.

[30]*Magnolia*, NS I (Dec., 1842), 329.

[31]*Views and Reviews*, I, 212. For following quotations, 214; 215-16.

[32]*Letters*, IV, 589. See also IV, 580.

[33]*Mellichampe*, 4-5. Raymond C. Palmer, *The Prose Fiction Theories of William Gilmore Simms* (Unpub. Dissertation, Indiana University, 1946), 41, notes that "Simms nowhere makes a concise definition of his meaning of design," and gave it major importance only in "Modern Prose Fiction" (*SQR, XV* [April, 1845], 41-83). But he adds: "*Design* is used in this paper because Simms employs it more often than other words of similar meaning, such as "*imagination, creative imagination, constructive imagination, concept*, and *fabric*. . . . The design is composed of two parts: the purpose of the artist in creating his work of art and the over-all plan by which he means to carry out his purpose." For Palmer's discussion of design, see pp. 41-45. Alexander Cowie, Introduction, *The Yemassee*, xxiv, prefers the word *invention*.

[34]*Letters*, III, 242n. Simms admitted (*The Wigwam and The Cabin*, 4)

that he found it "much easier to invent a new story than to repair the defects of an old one."

[35]*Views and Reviews*, I, 218.

[36]*SQR*, XV (April, 1849), 74-75. In the Introduction to *Confession*, p. 7, he admitted that "The work grew beneath his hands to a size far exceeding his original purpose. . . . A work so growing, without design, may be strictly legitimate, as the natural progress of the author's mind to the solution of his problem, yet fail in every essential, as a work of interest for the reader, or even of art. The mere logical array of facts, distribution and arrangement of the proper relations of parties and events—all these, however well done, may yet constitute no more claim to art than may be urged in behalf of a well-put law argument."

[37]*Letters*, IV, 168, 191n.

[38]*Letters*, II, 308. This would preclude digressions, but would not preclude moral or philosophical commentary by the author, who will "strive to rise from his mere narrative—he will pause in the analysis of character—he will linger in contemplation of the beautiful and noble, and will strive to persuade, or compel, his reader to linger and enjoy it also." "Bulwer's Genius and Writings," *Magnolia*, NS I (Dec., 1842), 331.

[39]*Letters*, I, 316.

[40]*Letters*, V. 207.

[41]*Letters*, I, 400. In *Confession*, 124, although speaking through a fictional character, he strikingly phrased this belief: "The genius that suffers itself to be fettered by the *precise*, will perhaps learn how to polish marble, but will never make it live, and will certainly never live very long itself."

[42]*Letters*, II, 528.

[43]*SQR*, XVII (July, 1850), 360.

[44]*Magnolia*, NS I (Dec., 1842), 331-32.

[45]*Idem.*

[46]Preface, *The Partisan*, viii.

[47]Quotations in this paragraph are from *The Magnolia*, NS I (July, 1842), 51-52.

[48]*SQR*, XV (April, 1849), 41-83. Very late in life, he again stated this belief, in "The Cub of the Panther," *The Old Guard* (1869), VII, 815: Tell "the whole *truth*, and nothing but the truth; 'nothing extenuate,' and 'nothing set down in malice'; and the moral grows inevitable. It is always present in the perfect fiction."

[49]Advertisement, *Mellichampe*, 5-6.

[50]*Letters*, I, 255-57. Also in *The Magnolia*, III (Aug., 1841), 376-80.

[51]*Letters*, I, 265. Also in *The Magnolia*; see above note.

[52]*Letters*, I, 258-59.

[53]Cowie, Introduction, *The Yemassee*, xxiii-xxv.

[54]*SQR*, XV (April, 1849), 72-73. Simms frequently emphasized the need for "naturalness": "what is fiction, but the nice adaptation, by an artist, of certain ordinary occurrences in life, to a natural and probable conclusion. . . . The naturalness must be that of life as it is shown in such picturesque situations as are probable—seemingly real—and such as the artist has chosen for his guide. . . . We require as close reasoning, and deductions as logically drawn, in tale and novel, as in a case at law or in equity. . . . What we show must not only be the truth, but it must also seem like the truth" (*The Wigwam and the Cabin*, 71-72).

[55]See, in order named, *SQR* (April, 1849), XV, 83; *Letters*, I, 154; *Views and Reviews*, I, 213-14, and II, 151.

[56]*Views and Reviews*, I, 215.

[57]*Ibid.,* I, 33. In the published version of "The Moral Character of Hamlet" (*Orion,* IV, 89) he states flatly that *The Fair Maid of Perth* is "the most *artistical,* beyond comparison, of any of the romances of its author." But in the later revised and unpublished manuscript in the Charles Carroll Simms collection in the South Carolina Library, he modified his earlier high praise to "one of the most ingenious of the many wondrous legends of the author."

[58]W. P. Trent, *William Gilmore Simms,* 7; quoted from Hayne's article in the *Southern Bivouac,* NS I (Oct., 1885), 261.

[59]See particularly chs. XXI-XXII and XLV.

[60]*Views and Reviews,* I, 223 and II, 161, 175.

[61]*Views and Reviews,* II, 161-62, 175. Quotations in following paragraph from pp. 174, 175, and 165, in that order.

[62]*SQR,* NS IX (Jan., 1854), 224-28. In *Views and Reviews,* II, 159-60, he declares roundly: "There is something decidedly unfriendly to art, in the present popular mode of writing for *serial* publication. . . . The author soon becomes indifferent to all general proportions in his work,—to all symmetry of outline,—all compactness of plan and execution. He uses irrelevant matter,—forgets or neglects his main purpose,—yields to frequent changes of plan—to frequent weariness,—and, satisfied in the preparation of a few spirited sketches, such as may keep attention wakeful,—becomes heartily indifferent to consistency of tone, harmony of parts and colour, uniformity of execution, or appropriate finish and denouement. The winding up of plots, framed in this manner, is usually feeble and defective. . . . It is the fault of the whole tribe,—Dickens, Ainsworth, and the rest."

[63]*SQR,* XV (April, 1849), 270.

[64]On *Hard Times,* a "Lorris" Letter, Charleston *Mercury,* Dec. 29, 1854; *SQR,* XIX (April, 1851), 568. Reviewing *A Tale of Two Cities* in the Charleston *Mercury,* May 9, 1860, Simms wrote that "Mr. Dickens cannot make a dull book, though he may sometimes lead his readers into the long-drawn-out meshes of a tedious one." Simms thought it "less artistlike" and "less profound and unique, than his average performances—still the interest of the reader is maintained throughout."

[65]*SQR,* XIX (Jan., 1851), 74-100.

[66]*SQR,* XIX (April, 1851), 559.

[67]Review of *The Newcomes* in Charleston *Mercury,* Feb. 26, 1856.

[68]Charleston *Mercury,* Jan. 5, 1860.

[69]*Views and Reviews,* II, 168.

[70]Charleston *Mercury,* Jan. 5, 1860.

[71]*SQR,* N. S. VII (April, 1853), 515, 521-22; VIII (July, 1853), 266. In the Charleston *Mercury,* Jan. 5, 1860, Simms wrote that Thackeray's "stories are all excellent specimens of mental joinery and construction. The parts fit beatifully. . . . Symmetry, propriety, a nice adaptation of means to ends; perfect fitness of action to character, and of character to plan; keen insight of the social moral; a judgment that rarely errs in the proper sentiment for his parties, or proper person for his agent; or a proper *denouement* for his piece; these are among his chief excellences as an author of fiction."

[72]*Magnolia,* NS I (Dec., 1842), 329-45.

[73]*Ibid.,* 329.

[74]*Letters,* II, 227.

[75]*SQR,* NS VIII (July, 1853), 266; *Magnolia,* NS I (Dec., 1842), 332. As early as 1829, Simms had praised *The Disowned* and *Pelham* (*Southern Literary Gazette,* I, Feb., 1829, 321-23): "The author writes well, and is

evidently a man of first rate genius. . . . We think the conception of
character over-charged and extravagant, but the execution excellent." After
the war, Simms wrote brief notices of various reprints of Bulwer's works.
Ernest Maltravers had survived thirty years; it was a good minor novel,
but not "entitled to rank in the same category with a production like
the 'Wilhelm Meister' of the great German author" (Charleston *Courier*,
June 9, 1868). In two round-up reviews (May 25, 1868 and August 24, 1868)
of recent reprints, Simms stressed that Bulwer had been especially successful in "blending the novel with the romance." Other Bulwer notices
appeared in the *Courier* on June 29, 1868; Sept. 22, 1868; and Dec. 9, 1868.
[76]*SQR*, VII (April, 1845), 312-49. Quotation on p. 348.
[77]*Ibid.*, 344-45.
[78]*SQR*, XV (April, 1849), 70-72. Simms adds, however, that while Lever's
later novels show a greater mastery of construction and design, they have
less vigor than his earlier work. In reviewing *Gerald Fitzgerald*, "*The
Chevalier*," in the mockcourt atmosphere that he created for the "Literary
Docket," Charleston *Mercury*, June 21, 1859, Simms charges that Lever,
"a rollicking Irishman," had "changed his deportment in almost as many
books as he had written; at one moment appearing as a 'Bould Dragoon';
at another as a sentimental fighting Hamlet or Romeo; now dashing into
broad farce, fun and comedy; now as full of horrors as MacBeth or
Richard Crookback." After the war, in the Charleston *Courier*, Nov. 4,
1868, he called *The Bramleighs of Bishop's Folly* agreeable and interesting,
with nothing in it to startle or shock.
[79]*Views and Reviews*, II, 164. In the Jan., 1852, *SQR* (NS V, 263) he complained also of monotony: "crime is committed, the innocent is accused,
and is only saved, at the last minute, by the guilty man turning up. The
action and interest in seven out of ten of his tales have hinged upon
this single condition." But James' novels were always "readable."
[80]*SQR*, NS VII (April 1853), 515. As early as July, 1842 (*Magnolia*, NS
I, 53-56) Simms had called James a "most prolific writer" and "as a mere
raconteur," about the best in England. Even then, Simms was complaining
that James' works were alike. He had succeeded in imitating Scott "only
in one of the attributes of that great intellect:—In warming the interest
of his reader in the progress of the history."
[81]*Letters*, III, 425 n.
[82]*Letters*, IV, 73-74. The notice referred to in Simms' letter to James was
a brief review in the Charleston *Mercury*, July 3, 1858, of *Lord Montagu's
Page*.
[83]*SQR*, XV (April, 1849), 41-83. See especially p. 75. Simms objected
vigorously to the sentimental and immoral novels of Lamartine and
George Sand—perverted work that had been heavily influenced, like so
much of French fiction, by the bad but powerful work of Rousseau. *See
SQR*, XVII (July, 1850), 355-69. In the *Southern Patriot*, Oct. 8, 1845, he
complained that Sue's *Wandering Jew* contained "an insidious, and only
partially disguised attack on the rites of marriage," and attributed a good
part of his popularity in America to his "vigorous crusade against Roman
Catholicism, especially the Jesuits." Dumas, amazingly, in spite of interesting
parts and good points, sometimes allowed "his historical material to fetter
his prerogatives as a romancer. . . . To write a really good historical
romance, the author should be careful to make his chronicles subordinate
to his persons—to use history sparingly, and only as tributary to the main
object of developing individual character, under striking conditions,
and with a view to the finest dramatic effects" (Charleston *Mercury*, Feb.
3, 1855).

[84]Respectively, "Goethe's Essays on Art," *Southern and Western Magazine*, II (Dec., 1845), 423-24 and the *Correspondence Between Schiller and Goethe*, 424; *Southern Literary Gazette*, I, March 1829, 384-85; *SQR*, XX (July, 1851) 248. In *SLG*, he quotes the "admirable analysis of the character of 'Hamlet' " from the novel. In 1851 he praised Carlyle's translation highly, and lamented that there was no good American edition of Goethe's works.

[85]*Southern and Western*, II (Nov., 1845), 357-58.

[86]*SQR*, XV (April, 1849), 78; XVII (April, 1850), 255; NS VIII (July, 1853), 267.

[87]*SQR*, XIX (April, 1851), 548; *Letters*, III, 109. In an obituary notice of Charlotte Brontë, Charleston *Mercury*, May 1, 1855, he again praised her highly as a writer of fiction.

[88]"Literary Docket," Charleston *Mercury*, June 22, 1859; Charleston *Courier*, April 13, 1869. Writing on *Phineas Finn*, Simms notes that it "is not liable to objections sometimes urged, that of giving false views of life and characters."

[89]Respectively, Charleston *Mercury*, May 20, 1859; Charleston *Mercury*, Oct. 3, 1860; Charleston *Courier*, Aug. 31, 1866. Here Simms complains that in all her novels there is "a residue of unpleasantness." Briefly noticing a reprint of *Romola* (Charleston *Courier*, Nov. 11, 1869), Simms attributes its success to "exquisite characterization" rather than to the "dramatic nature of the incident," although he adds that it is "full of beauty."

[90]*Views and Reviews*, I, 216-22.

[91]*Ibid.*, 212, 225.

[92]*SQR*, XVI (Oct., 1849), 269-70. In "A Chat in a Symposium," *Cosmopolitan*, I 19-21, Simms and his fellow-editors (Charles Rivers Carroll and Edward Carroll) discuss Scott and Cooper. Both novelists, for all their genius, were cursed with too much facility, and had done too much hasty work at the demand of publishers and readers. Cooper in the *Heidenmauer* (1832) had erred in choosing a foreign subject; he had succeeded better in his American novels because "Long and familiar contemplation of his own country and its associations, admirably prepared him for their illustrations." See John C. Guilds, Jr., "William Gilmore Simms and the *Cosmopolitan*," in *Georgia Historical Quarterly*, XLI, 31-41.

[93]*Southern Literary Gazette*, I (Sept., 1828), 8.

[94]*The Cosmopolitan*, I, 14-15.

[95]*Letters*, I, 144.

[96]*The Damsel of Darien*, 9.

[97]*Views and Reviews*, II, 177. Simms prefaces the following quotation by noting that Paulding "enjoys considerable American reputation as a humorist," but that he had "never esteemed him greatly in this character." *Southern Patriot*, May 4, 1847. See also *Southern and Western*, II (Sept., 1845), 216.

[98]*Letters*, I, 147.

[99]*Letters*, I, 67. Simms' objection that Bird made his characters talk alike has been noted earlier.

[100]*Southern Patriot*, March 10, 1846.

[101]*Letters*, III, 122.

[102]*Letters*, III, 183-84.

[103]*SQR*, XXI (April, 1852), 530, and XXII (July, 1852), 203-220. In the second article, Simms adds (p. 220) after the word *favorites*: "whom we hold in great respect as an author, and in great regard as a man."

[104]*The Wigwam and the Cabin*, 39. In Ch. I of "The Two Camps,"

Simms explains that his character and Horse-Shoe "were drawn from not dissimilar sources."

[105]*Southern Patriot*, July 20, 1846.

[106]*Letters*, II, 174-75.

[107]*Letters*, II, 42-43.

[108]*Idem.*

[109]*Southern and Western*, II (Dec., 1845), 426.

[110]*Southern Patriot*, March 2, 1846.

[111]*Letters*, II, 99.

[112]*SQR*, XX, 265-66 (July, 1851); *SQR*, XXII (Oct., 1852), 543.

[113]Charleston *Mercury*, June 7, 1860. In *The Marble Faun*, the major defect is that Hawthorne had "a too great desire to make not only a story, but a picturesque survey of Italy," but it will richly repay those readers, especially, whose views are "somewhat metaphysical."

[114]Perry Miller, *The Raven and the Whale* (1956), 107, 147. See also John Stafford, *The Literary Criticism of "Young America"* (1952). Although Simms was aware of the personal criticism rampant in his day, he did not approve of it; he wrote to James Lawson that "criticism now-a-days does not so much depend upon the book as upon the author. It is the man, not the volume, that is most commonly under the knife" (*Letters*, I, 100).

[115]*Letters*, I, 440.

[116]*Letters*, V, 55.

[117]*Southern Patriot*, April 9 and 25, 1846. Miller, *op. cit.*, 158, considers, I think erroneously, these reviews as "the faithful Simms, obeying orders" given by Duyckinck. Miller, evidently unaware of how long Simms had advocated nationalism in literature, exaggerates Simms' subservience to the "Young America" group.

[118]*SQR*, XVII (July, 1850), 514-20.

[119]*SQR*, XVII (April, 1850), 259-60.

[120]*SQR*, XVI (Oct., 1849), 260.

[121]*SQR*, XXI (Jan., 1852), 262.

[122]*SQR*, XXII (Oct., 1852), 532.

[123]*SQR*, XXII (July, 1852), 261.

[124]*SQR*, XVI (Oct., 1849), 245-46.

[125]*Southern and Western*, I (June, 1845), 434-35; *Letters*, V, 388. In the "Literary Docket," Charleston *Mercury*, Aug. 20, 1859, he praised the purity of her "taste and style, the simplicity and grace of the writer, the quiet domestic interest . . . the just moral developed; and the general good sense, spirit and propriety" of the novelist.

[126]"Our Literary Docket," Charleston *Mercury*, July 12, 1859; Charleston *Courier*, June 4, 1867. In the earlier review, Simms mentions De Forest's two travel books. A social story like *Seacliff* especially requires invention, "if only to lessen the monotony of scenes in ordinary life."

[127]*Letters*, II, 29. The following quotations appear, in order, on II, 96, 105, 117. In *The Magnolia*, NS II (June, 1843), 391-400, Simms praised *The Career of Puffer Hopkins* as an attempt "to produce a book which should be characteristic and national in its features."

[128]*Views and Reviews*, II, 147, 151.

[129]*Letters*, IV, 168-69, 181, 191n.

[130]*Letters*, IV, 181. Simms believed this to be an important function of the critic: "He is bound to point out faults—if his discrimination is adequate to such a duty; and, if not, he had better go through a course of Pope's Essay on his own art" ("American Criticism and Critics," *Southern Literary Journal*, II (July, 1836), 396.

[131]Charleston *Mercury*, Jan. 20, 1860. After the war Simms wrote various notices of new works by Cooke. In the Charleston *Courier*, May 22, 1867, he praised *Surry of Eagle's Nest* for its rapid movement, vigorous action, effective scenes, and graphic incident, but qualifies this by noting that the "narrative, which is wonderfully full, free, and flowing," runs away with Cooke, and makes him too little heedful of his characterization. In the *Courier*, May 29, 1868, he wrote that *Fairfax* "is one of many graceful, sprightly, and very spirited tales, which he has written, illustrative of old times, old manners, lovely scenes, and startling incidents, in the history of the 'Old Dominion'." But Cooke was forced by necessity to write far too rapidly—"a pitiable fate for the author—the poet—the artist."

[132]Charleston *Courier*, Nov., 4, 1868.

[133]Charleston *Courier*, Feb. 4, 1868. In a letter to Lawson the year before (*Letters*, V, 88) written on the back of a "Prospectus of *Southern Society*," Simms called attention to its "formidable list of writers." Among these were Simms, Cooke, Timrod, Hayne, and Lanier.

[134]*Martin Faber*, I, 154. See H. H. Clark, "Changing Attitudes in Early American Literary Criticism," in Floyd Stovall (ed.), *The Development of American Literary Criticism* (1955), 52.

[135]See R. H. Fogle, "Organic Form in American Criticism: 1840-1870," in Stovall, *op. cit.*, 65, 82-83. As Fogle notes, this organic concept has recently been perceptively described in Arthur Lovejoy's *Great Chain of Being* (1936).

[136]*Views and Reviews*, I, 214-15.

[137]*Ibid.*, I, 25.

Chapter III   NOTES: ON POETRY AND POETS

[1]*Letters*, III, 275.

[2]*Letters*, IV, 422.

[3]*Letters*, 275, 262.

[4]*Letters*, I, 223. This is really the second part of an article on Southern Literature, although in the form of a letter to the editor; it was published in *The Magnolia*, III (Feb., 1841) 69-74. Here Simms objects to imitative poetry, and states that no American poet deserves "the glorious epithet of 'Builder'" (p. 216)—a favorite expression with him. In *Views and Reviews*, II, 147-48, he compares a poem to a building, and the poet's "faculty as a *builder* [is] the highest evidence, perhaps, of poetical endowment."

[5]*Letters*, IV, 454.

[6]*Letters*, IV, 616. This was written to the poet Charles Warren Stoddard, Oct. 24, 1866, giving an evaluation of Stoddard's poetry, and advising him to study Tennyson less, and Shakspeare, Milton, and Dryden more. In "A Few Words about Poetry," in the Columbia *Phoenix*, April 21, 1865, Simms had written that "Poetry is essentially *winged* thought." In a review appraising Macaulay's "thoughtful, instructive, and eminently valuable historical and philsophical essays" (Charleston *Mercury*, Feb. 20, 1856), Simms recorded his own belief that "philsosophy only does mole-fashion, what poetry does eagle-fashion." But he added that the truth "is attainable, by the honest worker, in either region."

[7]Trent, 7; *Letters*, III, 261. Earlier he had limited his claim: "I regard poetry as my forte, particularly in the narrative and dramatic forms" (*Letters*, II, 257).

[8]See Hayne's letter to Taylor in *The Correspondence of Bayard Taylor and Paul Hamilton Hayne*, ed. by Charles Duffy (1945), 94-95; and D. M. McKeithan, *A Collection of Hayne Letters*, 428. However, in a review of

Simms' poems in *Russell's Magazine*, II, 152-60, Hayne compared Simms' poetry with that of the Elizabethan dramatists in its "directness of diction, its abrupt audacity and defiance of conventional trammels, its compressed vigor."

[9]*Letters*, I, 221-22. There are five mss. of "Poetry and the Practical" in the Charles Carroll Simms Collection. An 80-page ms., dated Jan. 4, 1851, was delivered as a lecture in Augusta, Georgia. The second ms. adds little. Simms then revised and enlarged, until he had three mss. of 46 pages, 32 pages, and 50 pages. These were delivered as three lectures in Charleston, May-June, 1854. Page references in the text without Roman numerals refer to the single lecture; with Roman numerals, to the three lectures. In III, 41, Simms marked through Virgil, and substituted Horace.

[10]*Letters*, III, 225; first published in *The Magnolia*, III, 69-74. I have treated Simms' belief that only professional writers could produce enduring literature in the section on Nationalism and Sectionalism.

[11]Letters, IV, 432. In the Dedication to *Areytos, or Songs of the South* (1846), Simms had described his lyrics as improvisations inspired by "the spontaneous emotion, the sudden flight of fancy, or the voluntaries of sentiment and passion. We must take such performances as so many short bird-flights."

[12]In the review in *Russell's*, II, 159, Hayne notes that Simms had an "apparently invincible repugnance to the distasteful duty of correction."

[13]Trent, 145-50. Here Trent is considering *Grouped Thoughts and Scattered Fancies* (1845): "There are eighty-four of these quatorzains—for with a few exceptions they cannot be called sonnets." Trent's criticism is somewhat invalidated by his pedantic definition of a sonnet, and more by his statement that he is interested in using the poems to illustrate the defects of Southern poetry. A reader less interested in proving a point may well think that some of the poems are interesting and stimulating.

[14]*Southern Patriot*, July 31, 1860.

[15]Charleston *Courier*, April 5, 1867. This is a review of *The Book of the Sonnet* (1867), edited by Leigh Hunt and S. Adams Lee. The commentary on American sonnets is by Paul Hamilton Hayne and George Henry Boker. The following quotations are from this article. Simms enjoyed speculation about the indebtedness of Spenser to Sidney, and of Elizabethan sonnet-writers to Wyatt and Surrey, and eventually to Petrarch and Dante.

[16]In October, 1855, Simms asked a correspondent for news of Boker and Thomas Buchanan Read, "bright and shining lights of literature in the empire of Quakerdom," (*Letters*, III, 407). Although he liked Boker and admired his works, he probably in this over-praise was thinking only of comparing Boker with writers of sonnets, since he was reviewing an anthology limited to that genre. Simms published a favorable review of *Konigsmark* in the Charleston *Courier*, Nov. 6, 1869, in which he repeated that, although not popular, Boker was an excellent poet and playwright. [17]*Letters*, V, 356.

[18]*Letters*, III, 169. Perhaps Simms over-states his point, since the letter is to Thomas Holley Chivers. However, in the ms. of "Poetry and the Practical," 70, he asserts: "Mere verse-making constitutes but a small part of the poetic faculty."

[19]*Letters*, I, 155. Possibly Simms' qualification should be noted: "At least I have sought to make it such, and as such I require that it should be judged." In his review of Wordsworth (*SQR*, NS II [Sept., 1850], 4-7), Simms discusses possible definitions of poetry, and decides there are no hard-and-fast rules for determining where prose ends and poetry begins,

and vice versa. He frequently praised a prose-writer for having poetical qualities: for example, De Quincey is described as a "remarkable essayist, endowed equally with the Poetical and the Metaphysical faculties" (Charleston *Mercury*, Feb. 6, 1855).

[20]*Letters*, III, 170.

[21]*Letters*, V, 409-10.

[22]*Letters*, II, 257.

[23]*Letters*, IV, 443. In *Views and Reviews*, I, 37, he calls Wordsworth "probably the greatest contemplative poet that has ever lived."

[24]Simms, *Poems Descriptive, Dramatic, Legendary, and Contemplative*, 154-57. Simms omits Dryden from his "Heads of the Poets," but considering how often he links "Shakspeare, Milton, and Dryden," there seems good reason for putting Milton second and Dryden third in his ranking of the English poets.

[25]*Ibid.*, 159.

[26]*Views and Reviews*, I, 37-40.

[27]Simms' longest and best treatment of Wordsworth is in his "Poetical Works of Wordsworth," SQR, NS II (Sept., 1850), 1-23. Part of the essay is devoted to Henry Taylor. The above quotations are from this essay, and from SQR, NS II (Nov., 1850), 540. But Simms constantly uses Wordsworth as a touchstone by which to judge contemplative poets. In the *Columbia Phoenix*, June 15, 1865, Simms in an article, "Wordsworth on Taste and Culture," especially praised the English poet for being inspired by nature unadorned, and not prettified. In *Letters*, II, 137, he praised Wordsworth and Bryant for "associating the moral with the physical."

[28]"Wordsworth on Literature," in the Columbia *Phoenix*, June 21, 1865.

[29]SQR, NS II, (Sept., 1850) 22-23.

[30]*Ibid.*, 11: SQR, NS X (Oct., 1854), 535; SQR XVI (Oct., 1849), 260. In *Letters*, I, 282, he wrote Lawson: "I am not so sure that you do not underrate Cowper." Simms notes occasionally the evil influence that French poetry had on English, during and after the Restoration; in *Views and Reviews*, I, 90, he deprecates "the substitution, in England, of French for English poetry—the clinquant of a false, for the hearty ring of the genuine metal."

[31]*Ibid.*, 22.

[32]*Idem.* In the Charleston *Courier*, April 29, 1868, under the title "Robert Southey's Work," Simms welcomed a reprinting of his work.

[33]*Letters*, I, 12. Simms refers to Sir Philip Sidney, and adds that he does not see "any reason for his enthusiasm" for the old ballads. But Byron had some kinship with the balladwriters: his "egotism and passion—his vain pride—his intense kindlings—his stubborn resolution not to do right because his enemies censure his wrong doing—declare the genuine English character" (*Views and Reviews*, I, 39).

[34]Simms, *Poems*, II, 158.

[35]As late as 1868, Simms was comparing certain of his poems with Byron's as "not descriptive but dramatic, passionate, not contemplative. . . . It is quite as coherent and as much a tale as the Giaour" (*Letters*, V, 151-52).

[36]In a review, "Montgomery's Messiah," *Magnolia*, IV (Jan., 1842), 6.

[37]*The Wigwam and the Cabin*, 71.

[38]*Magnolia*, IV, 6.

[39]*Views and Reviews*, I, 82-83.

[40]Simms, *Poems*, II, 158.

[41]*Views and Reviews*, I, 96.

[42]*Poems*, II, 157-58.

[43]*The Forayers*, 235. Dennison certainly had "his own artless manner"— a phrase that Simms perhaps injudiciously applies to Burns.

[44]*Views and Reviews*, I, 40.

[45]In *Letters*, V, 88, he amusingly paraphrases Keats' *Endymion*: "it is a *thing of Promise*, which on a Bank Note, is a thing of Beauty, and so, as Shelley sings, a joy forever."

[46]*Letters*, V, 267. He also asked for a copy of Coleridge's work.

[47]Simms, *Poems*, II, 159.

[48]*Southern Literary Gazette*, I (Sept., 1828), 42. The review (41-47) objects to Hunt's making himself the most important character in the book, and to his reducing Byron to "a level low indeed." Mr. Duncan Eaves ("An Early American Admirer of Keats," *PMLA*, LXVII [Sept., 1952], 895-98) thinks the tone "unmistakably Simms's." I agree, but the entire article cannot be by Simms, for the reviewer notes that Lord Byron was fearless, "as we heard a very intimate friend of his say in London" (p. 43). James W. Simmons, his fellow-editor, may have written all the article, or the two editors may have written it together. Certainly Simms approved of the ideas on Keats and Shelley.

[49]In "The Love of Study," *Southern Literary Gazette*, NS I (May 15, 1829), 19. Simms quotes a sonnet "said to have been written by John Keats," but it has not been identified as by Keats. Simms also misquoted slightly two lines from "The Eve of St. Agnes" in "The Progress of Civilization," *American Monthly Magazine*, III (August, 1834), 365.

[50]*SQR*, NS II (Sept., 1850), 21; *SQR*, NS II (Nov., 1850) 535.

[51]*Letters*, V, 616.

[52]*Letters*, II, 416. Although not mentioned in this letter, Simms included Philip James Bailey and Henry Taylor in his "Heads of the Poets," *Poems*, II, 161.

[53]Simms, *Poems*, II, 159.

[54]*SQR*, NS II (Sept., 1850), 256-57.

[55]*Letters*, IV, 529.

[56]*Letters*, V, 150.

[57]Charleston *Courier*, Jan. 16, 1867. Apparently Simms did not see *The Queen Mother, Rosamond—Two Plays* (1860), until after he had read some later works. Probably his edition did not indicate that it was a reprint, for he assumed this was a new work. In the Charleston *Courier*, June 19, 1866, he writes that "Atalanta and Chastelard have been justly exceedingly praised and admired, and the present poem has many of the merits and all the defects of its predecessors . . . there is no sense of latent power in these poems."

[58]*SQR*, NS II (Sept., 1850), 233-47. In the *Southern Patriot*, Oct. 8, 1845, he called *Festus* "a book for your student of metrical metaphysics," and notes it was modelled after *Faust*.

[59]"Later Poems of Henry Taylor," *SQR*, XV (July, 1849) 484-526. See also *SQR*, NS II (Sept., 1850), 21, where he links Tennyson and Taylor as the "greatest poets now living in England," but the structure of their verse "depends upon the noble theory of Wordsworth's best practice." Also, they have received their philosophical ideas and mental discipline from Wordsworth.

[60]Simms, *Poems*, II, 160. But Simms noted unfavorably that Campbell "nibbled" some "fine lines" from Philip Freneau.

[61]*Southern and Western*, I (May, 1845), 358-59; Charleston *Mercury*, Feb. 16, 1860.

⁶²Charleston *Mercury*, May 24, 1860.

⁶³"Our Book Table," Charleston *Courier*, Feb. 24, 1866.

⁶⁴*The Partisan*, 390. In *Woodcraft*, 239, he notes incidentally that Thomas Gray's "The Bard" is "much undervalued . . . a production very far superior, in all poetic respects, to the over-lauded elegy of the same writer."

⁶⁵*The Scout*, 295. This foppish surgeon, Hillhouse, quotes pedantically and without much understanding from Milton, Pope, Shakspeare, and Ovid— pp. 298, 300, 325, 363.

⁶⁶*Eutaw*, 335. Simms objects especially to their use of "antiquated divinities" and artificial speech.

⁶⁷An amusing example (*Katharine Walton*, 62): a bibulous British officer says, to justify his consumption of Madeira and Jamaica: " 'Drink deep,' was the counsel of the little poet of Twickenham."

⁶⁸*Letters*, V, 174-77. Of the quotation from Milton's Sonnet XXII, he advises that Lawson's daughter Mary "look up this quotation in a book which I fear she never reads."

⁶⁹*Letters*, I, 367, and V, 105.

⁷⁰SQR, NS II (Sept., 1850), 15.

⁷¹*Letters*, I, 256, 265. Although couched in the form of a letter to the editor, this was really an article and was published in *The Magnolia*, III (Aug., 1841), 376-80.

⁷²"Copyright Law," *SLM*, X (Jan., 1844), 13.

⁷³SQR, NS IV (Oct. 1851), 538.

⁷⁴*Southern Literary Gazette*, I (Dec., 1828), 237-53. Simms also presents a qualified defense of Byron's moral and religious views, 250-51, 253.

⁷⁵"Montgomery's Messiah," *Magnolia*, IV (Jan., 1842), 1-14. A note to this article states that "this article was in great part written in 1832, when the Messiah was published." The earlier article appeared in the *Knickerbocker*, IV (Feb., 1834), 120-34, under the cumbrous but accurate title, "John Milton vs. Robert Montgomery. Or a Modest Comparison of Paradise Lost and Regained, of the One, with the Messiah, Now Published in the Sacred Annual, of the Other." All the quotations are from *The Magnolia*.

⁷⁶Homer also was one of these. Some poets, like Cowper and Gray, had "genius with little blood." Byron and Burns died young, with their passions unconquered. Simms opens the article cited above by quoting from Andrew Marvell, "that rough and sturdy citizen, and scarcely less rough and sturdy poet."

⁷⁷SQR, XVII (Oct., 1852), 544. See also SQR, XV, (April, 1849), 260-61, and XVI (Oct., 1849), 240, where in a review of Lowell's *Fable for Critics* he spoke of Emerson as "really half-witted." Simms was personally and critically exasperated by Lowell's judgments. However, he was personally on friendly terms with Margaret Fuller; in the *Southern Patriot*, July 9, 1846, he described her as "a woman of thought, who *feels* her subject, and is one of our most human and genial philosophers." Reviewing Thoreau's *Walden* after sectional as well as philosophical lines had tightened (Charleston *Mercury*, Feb. 8, 1855), Simms called it a "queer, well-written book" that revealed Thoreau as "carrying out the antique Puritan philosophy to its proper results, in all social matters." But Thoreau's "intellect we should greatly wrong, did we not describe it as one well calculated to inspire the respect and compel the watchful consideration of yours. His book is full of a speculative interest."

⁷⁸*Southern and Western*, II (Nov., 1845), 342-60, esp. 348-49. Simms reviewed *The Conduct of Life* in the Charleston *Mercury*, Jan. 29, 1861, and

re-stated his views: "Perhaps the chief merit of Carlyle and Emerson really consists in this. They re-*commend* to our ears a useful commonplace, which had fallen into vulgarity. They enforce an old moral by a new costume. They, briefly, allegorize the sermon and epigrammatize the truth. . . . [Emerson] is rather excursive than deep; and is suggestive rather than profound. You will read him with pleasure and profit, at times; and there is this advantage in his obscurities, that respecting him as a man of fine talents, he provokes you to study."

[79] *Letters*, I, 157-58.

[80] *Southern Literary Gazette*, I (Nov., 1828), 157-58, 192.

[81] *Letters*, V, 208.

[82] "W. C. Bryant," *Magnolia*, IV (April, 1842), 193-201, esp. 199-200. Simms practically drags in a compliment to Bryant in a novel (*Eutaw*, 150): after quoting "The groves were God's first temples," he adds that Nelly Floyd "had no knowledge of this beautiful chant of one of our best native poets."

[83] *Magnolia*, NS I (Sept., 1842), 191-92.

[84] Charleston *Mercury*, Dec. 13, 1859.

[85] *Letters*, V, 311-12.

[86] Charleston *Courier*, Feb. 26, 1870. After Bryant sent him a copy of the volume, Simms wrote a brief notice that appeared in the *Courier*, April 12, 1870. Simms wrote to Bryant praising its "manly simplicity, its directness of aim, the absence of all that might be involved and circuitous, and the avoidance of all effort, in any place, to *graft* yourself upon your original. . . . I rejoice, though I did not doubt, that you would choose the good stout, manly English heroic blank as your medium of translation. *That* is the great verse of our language" (*Letters*, V, 309). Of modern poets, only Tennyson with his "free and fresh rendering" might have given a better translation (Letters, V, 208).

[87] *Letters*, V, 150.

[88] *Southern and Western*, II (July, 1845), 67-8.

[89] Charleston *City Gazette*, June 30, 1830. This was in a review of James W. Simmon's *The Age of Rhyme*. Simms felt that Simmons had underrated Bryant and Halleck. Ten years later, however, he wrote Lawson (*Letters*, I, 172): "I fully agree with you that he is not to be spoken of in the same breath with Bryant."

[90] *Letters*, I, 172. He also thought that Halleck, "a natural aristocrat," disdained the popular judgment and partly for that reason wrote too little. Sometimes he wrote above the popular taste: "in his satire, the weapon he uses is the small sword, not the bludgeon. It is a polished blade, and, however mortal the thrust, did not mangle the victim." (*Letters*, V, 149-50).

[91] *Letters*, I, 172.

[92] *Southern and Western*, II (Nov., 1845), 347-49.

[93] *Letters*, II, 68.

[94] *Letters*, V, 263-64, and a review of Longfellow's *New-England Tragedies* in the Charleston *Courier*, Nov, 19, 1869: "These things are at once dull and feeble, lacking equally in power, pathos and poetry. The wonder is that Mr. Longfellow, who is confessedly an artist—much more decidedly artist than poet—should have exhibited the bad taste of choosing such themes, brutal, if not bald, for the latest exercise of his muse. But the greater wonder is that Mr. Longfellow should so blunder as to attempt the Drama at all."

[95] *Letters*, II, 74; II, 90; and I, 71, respectively.

[96] *Letters*, I, 233.

[97]Charleston *Mercury*, Nov. 22, 1855.
[98]*SQR*, NS II (Sept., 1850), 255-56, Charleston *Mercury*, Feb. 8, 1855.
[99]*Southern and Western*, II (Nov., 1845), 342-60.
[100]Charleston *Courier*, Dec. 30, 1848, and *SQR*, XVI (Oct., 1849), 239-42. See also *Letters*, II, 567.
[101]*Letters*, II, 467-69, and *Southern and Western*, II (Nov., 1845), 348-49.
[102]*Letters*, III, 414.
[103]Charleston *Mercury*, Feb. 24, 1860. Simms notes that *The Autocrat* "never reached us."
[104]*Letters*, III, 96-97.
[105]*SQR*, NS III (April, 1851), 563-64.
[106]*SQR*, NS VII (Jan., 1853), 265.
[107]Charleston *Courier*, April 5, 1867. See Jay B. Hubbell, "Five Letters from George Henry Boker to William Gilmore Simms," *Pennsylvania Magazine of History and Biography*, LXIII (Jan., 1939), 66-71.
[108]The quotation is from one of the "Lorris" Letters, Charleston *Mercury*, Dec. 22, 1854. See also *SQR*, NS VII (Jan., 1853), 265, and especially "Recent American Poets," *SQR*, XVI (Oct., 1849), 224-32. See also a letter to Taylor in *Letters*, III, 333-34.
[109]*SQR*, NS VIII (July, 1853), 284.
[110]*Letters*, II, 43, 90, and III, 170.
[111]*Southern Patriot*, March 2, 1846.
[112]*Southern Patriot*, Nov. 10, 1845. This article mainly defends Poe's lecture in Boston, but it also characterizes him as "an admirable critic . . . methodical, lucid, forcible;—well-read, thoughtful, and capable, at all times, of rising from the mere consideration of the individual subject, to the principles, in literature and art, by which it should be governed." Poe had criticized Longfellow and other Boston favorites; moreover, Poe's poetry was "too original, too fanciful, too speculative" to be grasped by the ordinary audience.
[113]*Letters*, III, 169-70.
[114]*Southern and Western*, II (Oct., 1845), 278-81. See also *Southern Patriot*, Aug. 7, 1845.
[115]*Letters*, III, 168-70; *SQR*, NS VIII (July, 1853), 273. In *SQR*, NS VII (Jan,. 1853), 265-66, he remarks that Chivers' *Eonchs of Ruby* "blush their own praise," but that the book must be "kept in lavender for future use."
[116]*The Complete Works of Thomas Holley Chivers*, I, 139. This volume of correspondence was edited by Emma Lester Chase and Lois Ferry Parks.
[117]*SLM*, IX (Dec., 1843), 715-20; *SQR*, V (Jan., 1844), 103-18. In letters to Duyckinck, Simms complained frequently of Mathews' perversity.
[118]Letter to Tuckerman, in *Letters*, III, 70-71. Simms valued Tuckerman much more highly as a writer of prose, and treated this in an extensive review-article, "Tuckerman's Essays and Essayists," *SQR*, NS I (July, 1850), 370-406.
[119]*SQR*, NS I (April, 1850), 261.
[120]*Letters*, III, 346-47. However, in a letter signed "Lorris," Charleston *Mercury*, May 30, 1856, Simms takes the editor to task for not reviewing at length Meek's *The Red Eagle*: "I do not like to see our native authors, even in their crude beginnings, passed over neglectfully in our domestic courts of criticism. . . . Mr. Meek has a fine imagination, a lively fancy, an excursive thought, and a grace and force of expression which with proper pains-taking must assure him of the highest excellence in style."
[121]*Letters*, II, 307-08, and III, 38. In "John Esten Cooke of Virginia" (Charleston *Mercury*, Oct. 21, 1859), Simms wrote that the two brothers

shared "in large degree, the poetical faculty," and regretted that John's "claims as a poet have been obscured . . . by his superior successes in prose." [122]This was an idea that Simms frequently stated. Probably the best essay embodying this idea is in Russell's Magazine, III (April, 1858), 36-37, in a review of Howard Caldwell's Poems. Caldwell had written perceptive essays for Russell's on French writers ("Beranger," I [April, 1857], 37-45; "Victor Hugo," I [June, 1857], 259-77), but Caldwell argued in them that poetry attained its maturity in the lyric, in which "the full glories of subjectivity appear" (I, 37), and that the lyric follows "the caprices of music, rather than the rules of art" (39). This view did not coincide with Simms' ideas. Moreover Caldwell's poetry is imitative, lacking in music, and sometimes downright prose, although it also reveals "the glow of youth, the warmth of a genial nature, the sympathies of a true humanity. . . . We say to Mr. Caldwell . . . You are only now preparing yourself to write poetry. But what you have written, assures us that you have poetry in you." Caldwell never forgave Simms for this review.
[123]See Jay B. Hubbell, The Last Years of Henry Timrod, 155-56, 167; Letters, II, 563-64; III, 352, 369. His most practical tribute was in editing an anthology of the writings of his fellow-townsmen, The Charleston Book (1845). But in the Preface he felt it necessary to stress that many pieces, being the work of amateur writers, have "that air of didactic gravity, that absence of variety, and of the study of artistical attributes" that professional writing should have. To compensate, the reader will find "a liveliness of fancy, a fluency of expression, and a general readiness of resource."
[124]"Recent American Poets," SQR, XVI (Oct., 1849), 224-32, esp. 228. See also Letters, II, 563-64, where Simms writes: "every poetaster of Charleston looks upon me as an enemy. Yet scarcely a Southron has ever received a kind word in the South, unless from my pen; and even [J. M.] Legaré is indebted to me for a genial notice."
[125]"The Writings of Washington Allston," SQR, IV (Oct., 1843, 363-414. On his poetry, see 381 ff. In praising Allston as a painter, Simms notes: "The great genius thinks rather of the work itself, than of its rewards" (390). Contrasting Allston with amateurs generally, Simms remarks that "Nothing, that we know, has ever come from amateur authorship, but dilettantism, affectation, pert pretense, and the most miserable conceit" (396). In A Supplement to the Plays of William Shakespeare, 5, Simms declares flatly that the young author or artist learns most from studying imperfect early works, thus acquiring "a proper idea of the toils, the obstacles, and the trials" that even the genius must undergo. He adds: "It is mere dilettantism alone, which shrinks from such a development—preferring only the knowledge of the perfect results of labor, without being troubled with its processes."
[126]Quoted in Trent, 297.
[127]Letters, V, 426.
[128]Letters, V, 97.
[129]Simms' tribute, "The Late Henry Timrod," was published in Southern Society, I (Oct. 12, 1867), 18-19; it is reprinted in Jay B. Hubbell's The Last Years of Henry Timrod, 153-65.
[130]Hubbell, 154-56, 158. In Letters, IV, 592, Simms commented on Timrod's lack of flexibility, and added: "He is one of the best of the Southern Poets, refined and highly polished, with fine meditative tone, and a pure and graceful fancy."
[131]Letters, V, 290. In this letter Simms advised Hayne that "you should, as

you could, make your reputation out of the story of Sappho. . . . The point, if you will remember, is the conflict between Sappho's passions and her intellect" (289). Apparently Hayne did not take the advice.
[132]To Hayne in *Letters* IV, 430-32. Simms was in part defending himself against Hayne's criticism of his own lyrics as fugitive poems. They were instead, Simms claimed, "*Happy inspirations.*"
[133]*Southern Patriot*, July 31, August 1, 2.
[134]*Letters*, IV, 540.
[135]Preface, *War Poetry of the South*, VI.
[136]*Letters*, III, 70.

CHAPTER IV   NOTES: DRAMAS AND DRAMATISTS

[1]*Letters*, II, 130-31. In the letters that he wrote from New York for Charleston newspapers, he frequently commented on plays and actors. In a series of 24 letters in 1845 called "The Transcript" (*Southern Patriot;* this letter is dated Sept. 23 and appeared on Sept. 26), he describes the Keans' performances in *As You Like It.* He had watched Kean act for fifteen years and thought him "well-informed, intelligent . . . of good taste . . . not destined by nature, nor prepared by art, to attain the glories of the paternal name." Simms also describes his pleasure in twice going to hear operas in French.
[2]*Letters*, II, 150. Ellen Tree opened the season, Feb. 2, 1846, as Mrs. Haller in William Dunlap's *The Stranger.*
[3]*Letters*, I, 134.
[4]*Letters*, I, 244. Simms is here talking about writing for publication rather than for the stage. He proposed to contribute one or two dramas annually to *Roberts Semi-Monthly Magazine*, "which you might transfer to the book from your pages."
[5]*Letters*, I, 428.
[6]On *Timon*, see *Letters*, III, 202, 215, 237. It was completed in 1852, but in 1860 (*Letters*, IV, 218) Simms complained that "I have written for Mr. Forrest, a new version of Timon, altering the denouement, and making considerable alterations and additions, with the view to its presentation on the stage. But this he has, still in MS."
[7]*Views and Reviews*, I, 47-48.
[8]*Letters*, II, 369. Simms published *Norman Maurice* in 1851, and *Michael Bonham* in 1852; he re-published *Norman Maurice* in his *Poems*, 1853. There he also published a revised version of *Atalantis*, with a prefatory note that "I am not satisfied that the dramatic form was appropriately adopted, since it leads to expectations which the character of the poem will scarcely satisfy." Simms acknowledged indebtedness to *Comus* and *The Tempest. Michael Bonham* was produced in Charleston, March, 1855. Parts of various plays were published in magazines: an extract from *Sylla* in the *Southern Literary Journal*, NS IV (Sept., 1838), 187-92; *Benedict Arnold* in *The Magnolia Weekly*, 1853. Slightly over one act of *Don Carlos*, in a multilated condition, is in the Charles Carroll Simms Collection. In 1845 Simms wrote Lawson (*Letters*, II, 93): "I have conceived the idea of altering for the stage the play of 'Locrine' imputed to Shakspeare, and have succeeded in manufacturing a first act, out of portions of the 1 & 2 of the original." Simms published this part under the title, "The Death of the British Brutus" (*Sartain's Union Magazine*, VIII [April, 1851], 249-53), with a note that he was submitting "the first act to the reader, as unique in itself, and totally independent of what succeeds." Simms wrote to

Lawson (*Letters*, I, 285) that "At 14 I wrote a tragedy called 'The Female Assassin'—you may readily conjecture the sort of stuff which followed such a title. . . . I have in my possession now a tragedy partly written when I was 17-18—founded on the apostacy of Count Julian. From the materials of this tragedy, my romance of Pelayo was evolved, and the sequel"—*Count Julian*. The play was rehearsed and announced in Charleston, but never presented (Trent, 46-7); it was submitted to Forrest, and rejected (*Letters*, I, 122). Portions of it were published in a Charleston magazine, *The Rambler*, Nov. 14-Dec. 28, 1843, as *Pelayo, a Dramatic Poem*. See also Furman E. McEachern, Jr., "European Influences on the Dramas of William Gilmore Simms" (Unpub. M. A. Thesis, University of South Carolina Library, 1953).

[9]*Letters*, II, 369, 392.

[10]Preface, *Michael Bonham*, 3.

[11]Ms. in the Charles Carroll Simms Collection, South Caroliniana Library, University of South Carolina.

[12]*Letters*, II, 356-59.

[13]*Letters*, II, 368-69. Simms added that if "the main scheme and incidents suit him, it will be easy to expand and elaborate any portions which he may think wanting in force and finish."

[14]*Border Beagles*, 80. In the *Southern Literary Gazette*, I (Sept., 1828), 54-55, Simms and Simmons as editors published an indignant article about the reception of Cooper, an American actor, in London. The article emphasized our need for a proper national pride. It probably was by Simmons, who had been in London; parts of it were drawn from English publications. Certainly Simms approved the ideas expressed in it.

[15]*Letters*, II, 187-88, 190.

[16]"Thoughts on Theatricals," *Southern Patriot*, Aug. 19, 20, 21, 1846. He thought Forrest the "creation of the popular theatricals." In *A Supplement to the Plays of William Shakespeare*, 10, he shifted the emphasis, but makes essentially the same point: "The great cause of the decline of modern theatricals, is to be found in the fact that the press has made the people familiar with the piece played; and those who attend the theatre, accordingly, go only to discriminate between the styles of actors—thus substituting one art for another—to witness the pageantry, hear the music, and see the company."

[17]"The Transcript," *Southern Patriot* (Letter 10, dated New York, 1845, late September or early October, since letter 9 appeared Sept. 26, 1845. I have used Simms' undated clipping).

[18]Trent, 199.

[19]C. Hugh Holman, "Simms and the British Dramatists," *PMLA*, LXV (June, 1950), 346-59, especially 351-52.

[20]Frances M. Barbour, "William Gilmore Simms and the Brutus Legend," *Midwestern Folklore*, VII (Fall, 1957), 159-62.

[21]*Woodcraft*, 369. Whether or not Simms meant Porgy to be a direct imitation of Falstaff is, fortunately, outside the scope of this work. Hampton M. Jarrell in "Falstaff and Simms's Porgy," *American Literature*, III (May, 1931), 204-12, presents strong evidence that Simms deliberately drew upon Shakspeare, and arrives at the conclusion that it "seems to me we are safe in saying that Simms did use Falstaff as 'a sort of painter's model.' " Hugh Holman disagrees sharply: "Those qualities which seem most essentially to be Falstaff's appear as surface artificialities in Porgy,—those qualities which seem most essentially to be Porgy's appear not at all in Falstaff." In *The Partisan*, 110, Simms directly compares

the two men: Porgy "rather amused himself with a hobby when he made food his topic, as Falstaff discoursed of his own cowardice without feeling it." Porgy compares himself with "the fat knight of Eastcheap" in *Eutaw*, 351. But Simms also wrote that in the Elizabethan play *Sir John Oldcastle*, the character of "Sir John Wrotham, who is meant to be a Falstaff, with the additional value of courage, might have been successful, but that Falstaff stood in his way. . . . [It] fails only as it reminds us that we have known Falstaff." (*Supplement to the Plays of William Shakespeare*, 89).

[22] Grace W. Whaley, "A Note on Simms's Novels," *American Literature*, II (May, 1930), 173-74. She also finds that Simms quoted six times from Scott and Shelley, five from Spenser and Wordsworth. See also a perceptive article by Edward P. Vandiver, Jr., "Simms's Border Romances and Shakspeare," *Shakespeare Quarterly*, V (Spring, 1954), 129-39.

[23] *Border Beagles*, 81.

[24] *Ibid.*, 138-43.

[25] *Ibid.*, 414-16. Horsey and assuredly Simms think that "in the reading of that passage, Forrest is clearly wrong:—'Hang out our banners!' he says with an exclamatory pause; then adds, 'On the outward walls,/ The cry is still they come.'—Now, why should he depart from the old style of reading, which is thus:—'Hang out our banners on the outward walls;/The cry is still they come!' Why should we suppose that the coming of the enemy is only announced on the outward walls? The cry is everywhere—the whole castle hears it. Macbeth himself announces it, he being *within the castle* at the time. In this reading the passage is without sense."

[26] *Border Beagles*, 312, 326. The man of genius, Simms felt, was obviously hampered by rules and conventions, but the American writer must imitate European models and compete successfully with the foreigner before "he may venture unchallenged into some glorious outlawry of his own." (*Views and Reviews*, II, 164).

[27] *Letters*, II, 34-5.

[28] *Letters*, II, 415, 431. See also *Richard Hurdis*, 73.

[29] Quoted in Jay B. Hubbell, *The Last Years of Henry Timrod*, 54.

[30] *Letters*, II, 62-63.

[31] "Shakspeariana," *Southern Literary Journal*, NS IV (Sept., 1838) 184-86. This and the October article were signed "Dramaticus."

[32] "Errors in Shakspeare's Tempest," *Southern Literary Gazette*, I (Nov., 1828), 186-87 and "Shakspeare—The Tempest," NS I, (Sept. 15, 1829), 202-04. This article and the one listed immediately above were drawn from the same notes, for the 1838 article repeats several items from the 1828 article. All the items that Simms discusses in this paragraph are from *The Tempest*. For Simms' troubles with printers, see as an example his remarks on Southern magazines, *Letters*, I, 196-208.

[33] "Shakspeariana," *Southern Literary Journal*, NS IV (Oct., 1838), 253-56.

[34] "Shakspeare Publications," in a "Lorris" letter, Charleston *Mercury*, Dec. 12, 1854. Many of Collier's conjectures and emendations seemed to him good. He also recommended that American Libraries acquire the publications of the Shakespeare Society, Percy Society, Hakluyt Society, etc.

[35] "The Authorship of Shakespeare," *Southern Society*, Oct. 26, 1867. Simms termed the parallelisms and analogies cited "ridiculous," although he freely granted Bacon's "acknowledged genius, wit and wisdom."

[36] *Letters*, I, 415. The article was published in *Orion*, IV (March-June, 1844) 41-51; 76-90; 105-19; 179-94. The two manuscripts are in the Charles Carroll Simms Collection, South Caroliniana Library, University of South Carolina. They do not differ significantly from the article.

[37]*Orion*, IV, 41-42. On outlawry, see text above, and Note 315. Simms started the lectures with the idea of the vitality of great works of literature: The "Poet supersedes the Biographer." He then discussed the idea that the English drama was in its infancy, and that the dramatist was mainly concerned with the spectators, not the readers.

[38]*Ibid.*, 42-43.

[39]*Ibid.*, 43-44, 77. In the lectures he also pointed out these inconsistencies.

[40]*Ibid.*, 44. Hamlet's incertitude and indecision are emphasized more strongly in the manuscript of the second lecture.

[41]*Ibid.*, 45. In the manuscript of the first lecture, Simms disagrees even more strongly with earlier authorities.

[42]*Ibid.*, 51. The article draws on Robert Burton's *Anatomy of Melancholy* to describe the type of melancholy by which such a nature is distinguished. This is dropped entirely from the lectures.

[43]*Ibid.*, 106-7. Simms gives a lengthy analysis of the action, 78 ff.

[44]*Ibid.*, 89, 118-19. The article ends with a long recapitulation (179-94)) of Hamlet's interview with his mother. Hamlet remains suspicious of everyone. In *Letters*, I, 414, Simms wrote a correspondent that "According to my notion, Hamlet was totally deficient in courage, and was never mad." In *Letters*, III, 277, he qualified earlier remarks: "The argument I think ingenious and plausible."

[45]*Views and Reviews*, II, 171.

[46]"Modern Prose Fiction," *SQR*, XV (April, 1849), 62.

[47]*Letters*, I, 259-63. Although in the form of a letter to the editor, this was a thoughtful and considered article on morality and realism in literature. It was published in *The Magnolia*, III (Aug., 1841), 376-80. After quoting from Massinger, Simms adds: "It would do our people, as well as our critics, a great good, if they would study the old writers, the great men of English literature. They would cease to confound substances and shadows, names and things. They would then discover an important distinction, which is not often made, between morality intrinsically considered, and conventional tastes. . . . They belong to the same class of gigantic moralists, by whom the Holy Bible was translated—a volume, that, in every page, offends against the petty tastes of petty people, and yet a volume, the darkest and the most unseeming pages of which are full of startling truths, and moralities the most tremendous and exacting."

[48]*Poems*, II, 309. Simms has Caius Marius say, "Dost thou not feel my presence, like a cloud, / Before my coming, Rome?"

[49]Given as a footnote, 175 n., to his poem, "Scene at Actium," *New Eclectic Magazine*, VI (Feb., 1870), 173-76. Simms, discussing the evil effects of the Restoration on English literature (*Supplement to the Plays of William Shakespeare*, 10), makes one exception: "That Dryden must be recognized as a redeeming worker in the more modern period, will not impair the justice of its general condemnation."

[50]*Letters*, III, 448; IV, 616.

[51]*Letters*, I, 256; III, 366, 396, 399, 401; V, 347.

[52]*Confession*, 135-36.

[53]*Trent*, 122-23.

[54]*Views and Reviews*, II, 153.

[55]*Ibid.*, 156-57.

[56]*Trent*, 135-36. *Letters*, II, 334, 336, 359, 392. Just how rapidly Simms expected to do the editing is uncertain, but he complained bitterly to Lawson (II, 341) that "It has been pretty hard work with me to do an act a day, and one of the plays consumed a full week." If Lawson will look at

the revised plays, "You will see a toil which will frighten you." Yet
in spite of this he wrote Lawson a few months later (*Letters*, II, 409) that
"I contemplate a new and revised edition of Shakspeare entire, for which
my studies for years have been silently preparing me." Twelve years
later, in listing his various dramatic writings, he added (*Letters*, IV, 218):
"I once proposed a new ed. of Shakspeare, but the plan did not attract
my publisher."

[57] *A Supplement to the Plays of William Shakespeare*: comprising the seven
dramas, which have been ascribed to his pen, but which are not included
with his writings in modern editions, namely: *The Two Noble Kinsmen*;
*The London Prodigal; Thomas, Lord Cromwell; Sir John Oldcastle; The
Puritan, or The Widow of Watling Street; The [sic] Yorkshire Tragedy;
The Tragedy of Locrine.* Edited, with Notes, and an Introduction to each
Play, by William Gilmore Simms. New York, 1848. A second edition was
published in 1855. Both editions were copyrighted by George F. Cooledge
and Brother.

[58] *The Shakespeare Apocrypha*, edited by C. F. Tucker Brooke (Oxford,
1908), 425, 426 (where he calls Simms a "blind follower" of Malone),
433-35. In his edition of fourteen plays Brooke includes the seven selected
by Simms.

[59] *Supplement*, 25.

[60] *Supplement*, 37. Simms followed the same policy with Malone's texts. Reviewing *The Shakespearian Reader* (*SQR*, XVI, Oct. 1849, 249-50), Simms
complained that the editor had expurgated heavily. This might be suitable
for children, but Simms felt sorry for any adult of either sex who feared
his or her morals might be hurt by reading "the naked Shakspeare."

[61] *Supplement*, 169. Other typical deletions may be noted, 165, and 173.

[62] *Supplement*, 12. If Simms knew or had seen Alexander Dyce's edition
of *Sir Thomas More* (1844) he does not mention it, although he dedicated
his collection to Dyce; by the standards expressed above, Simms would
have excluded it from his own work. Except for *Sir Thomas More*, he was
at least cognizant of the claims for all the plays included by Tucker Brooke,
and the only one that he added to Brooke's list was *George a-Greene*.
Simms may have leaned heavily on the critical opinions of other men, but
his list was conservative and sensible.

[63] *Supplement*, 7. Simms adds: "We have numerous illustrative examples of
this history in modern times, with which the reader is familiar. Who, for
example, ever looked to the feeble ballads of Walter Scott, poor imitations
of Monk Lewis, for the splendid creations of Marmion and Ivanhoe? Who,
in the boyish ditties and college exercises of Lord Byron, so cruelly but
justly cut up by Brougham, in the Edinburgh Review, would have looked
for signs of that genius which afterwards brought forth Manfred, Childe
Harold, and Cain?"

[64] Trent, 7, 45-47. Simms used this play as the basis for *Pelayo* and *Count
Julian.*

[65] *Supplement*, 45-46. He was in part influenced by the opinions of Tieck,
Schlegel, and especially of Lessing, "one of the soundest of German critics."

[66] *Supplement*, 153. The next quotation is on the same page, and the long
one from pp. 153-54. Simms' general remarks (not of course his quotations)
are just as pertinent to *Titus* as to *Locrine*, and in fact answer beforehand
many of the objections to including that play in the Shakspeare canon.
Simms gives Milton's condensation of the story from Geoffrey of Mon-
mouth; notes that Spenser used it in the tenth canto of the *Faerie Queen*;
and quotes at length from Michael Drayton's *Polyolbion* because Drayton

is "but little read—a sturdy native muse—who deserves more consideration than he finds."

[67]*Supplement*, 154. His supporting quotations follow, 154-58.

[68]*Supplement*, 13-14. A good summary is given by E. K. Chambers, *William Shakespeare*, I, 531-32. Kittredge, in *The Complete Works of Shakespeare*, 1409, says flatly: "The ascription to Fletcher and Shakespeare in the title page is undoubtedly correct."

[69]*Supplement*, 67-68. Only Schlegel's opinion that it was "unquestionably Shakspeare's" made Simms hesitate about dismissing it from the canon entirely. On p. 88, however, he objects that Schlegel's criticism is "wholly valueless," since he links as equally mature and equally worthy of Shakspeare "These biographical dramas . . . Sir John Oldcastle, Thomas Lord Cromwell, and the Yorkshire Tragedy—putting them all in the same category." Simms preferred to assign *A Yorkshire Tragedy* to Thomas Heywood (p. 142).

[70]*Supplement*, 87-89.

[71]*Supplement*, 117-18.

CHAPTER V.   NOTES: NATIONALISM AND SECTIONALISM

[1]Unnumbered pages a-b, *Southern Literary Gazette*, I (Sept., 1828). The Introduction follows immediately, 1-8. Before Simms was connected with it, Simmons edited it as *The Tablet, A Weekly Literary Gazette*. The editors state that friends encouraged them to change to monthly publication. For the best general survey of this subject, see Jay B. Hubbell, "Literary Nationalism in the Old South," in *American Studies in Honor of William Kenneth Boyd*, 175-220; of value although not completely reliable, is Rollin G. Osterweis, *Romanticism and Nationalism in the Old South*.

[2]*SLG*, I, 3. Simms continued to stress the importance of language, although he gave up the idea of a native dialect, for he believed that "Language is the mirror of the national mind; it reflects, and very accurately, in its history and progress, the national character, and whenever it loses its simplicity and truthfulness it becomes an index of national degradation" (Charleston *Courier*, March 16, 1866).

[3]*Southern Society*, Nov. 2, 1867. In an article, "American Literature as Influenced by English Literature," Nov. 23, 1867, Simms noted that Prescott and Longfellow were artistic but imitative; Lowell a "representative of the common American mind, as it exists and works in the Eastern states"; and that much good work was not recognized because it was not done in the metropolitan centers. Provincialism had made us dependent on England, until Irving had developed an exquisitely delicate vein of quiet and fresh humor in the employment of domestic history. Paulding portrayed common life at "a Dutchman's fireside." Of more herculean power, of bolder and freer conception, "Cooper had launched forth on the seas, and into the vast forests and prairies of the interior." But Simms added that there must be more growth and greater independence.

[4]Charleston, 1833, 5-15. Only two issues were published; the second issue was devoted entirely to fiction. The three editors chat about Scott and Cooper (17-24), and bewail their too-great facility. Cooper wastes his genius. Irving, with far less genius, works "more providently." But Cooper succeeded with his Indian and sea stories.

[5]*Letters*, I, 8-9. Hugh Swinton Legaré, classical scholar and distinguished lawyer, agreed with him: "Nothing is more *perilous*, in America, than to be too long *learning*, and to get the name of bookish" (Quoted in Jay B.

Hubbell, *The South in American Literature*, 266). Simms paraphrases Legaré's statement in a review of Matthew Arnold's *Essays in Criticism*, Charleston *Courier*, May 23, 1866.

[6]*Letters*, I, 144-45.

[7]*Letters*, II, 215. This letter-article was published in *The Magnolia*, III (Feb., 1841), 69-74.

[8]*Ibid.*, 216. American periodicals, he thought, "seldom offer any thing pretending to the name of criticism. If they do, it is in that bastard sort of criticism which is called comparative. They compare one work with another, and if it so happens that a publication is sent forth, to which, in their experience, there is no likeness, they very judiciously remain silent, and simply announce the publication—awaiting the time when some more venturesome brother, with more wit or less discretion, shall open his batteries of blame, or pour forth his pellets of puff and commendation. Analytic criticism—an intrinsic examination of a work—is never pretended to by these papers; and the most that is done by them is simply to announce the new work, with some vague remark, which means every thing and nothing, and concludes with recommending it to the public and their readers." He considers Poe at some length, and as a critic rarely guilty of "puffing. . . . He is harsh in his reviews of many of our popular writers, and allows none of their faults to escape him. He has his favorites, it is true, but his bias seems rather the result of intimacy and habitual deference, than of any mean or mercenary disposition to conciliate. So far from universally puffing, he does not often praise, and he discriminates more justly, where he does so, than all the rest of our periodicals." At the time he wrote this, Simms was still smarting from Poe's review of *The Partisan*. It is a good example of his attempt always to be objective in his judgments.

[9]*Ibid.*, 217. This did not keep him from admiring Irving as a writer, especially as an essayist. In *SQR*, NS III (April, 1851), 571, he called the *Sketch Book of Geoffrey Crayon, Gent.* perhaps the best of Irving's works: "The quiet grace of his style, the delicacy and simplicity of his tastes, his happy sense of propriety, and his vein of fancy, at once pleasing and yet unobtrusive, all combine to render the essay his most favorite province." See *Letters*, V, 428-30, for his official tribute sent in 1860 to the Committee arranging the Irving Birthday Dinner.

[10]*Letters*, I, 220-21.

[11]*Ibid.*, 225.

[12]*Views and Reviews*, 143-46.

[13]"Ingraham's Writings," Charleston *Mercury*, Aug. 11, 1860. Simms uses the works of a highly popular novelist to retrace the history of novel publication in the United States. Simms noted his qualities as writer: "a pleasant style, an easy, attractive manner, a ready appreciation of the piquant and picturesque, and the somewhat too free use of the melodramatic, constituted the principal attraction in his writings; opposed to which, as a natural consequence of such hot haste to please the pleasant public, was a frequently crude conception, careless design, spasmodic action, exaggeration of tone, and a loose and careless style of utterance." Simms noted Ingraham's change to writing religious novels and defended his right to invent where the Bible is silent: it may be bad policy in that he risks offending popular taste, but "it is not an offence in *art.*"

[14]See Perry Miller, *The Raven and the Whale*, and John Stafford, *The Literary Criticism of 'Young America.'* Simms' letters to Duyckinck and Lawson in this period give the best picture of his ideas and position.

[15]For example, he wrote to Lawson in 1859 (*Letters*, I, 156): "With regard

to the course of the Knickerbocker, I believe I have already told you that I am dissatisfied with it. Its notices of my books for the last three years have been positively unfavorable, or the Editor has slurred over their claims in a brief paragraph in which he avowed himself not to have read them or something of similar sort."

[16]*Letters*, II, 41-42.

[17]*Letters*, V, 388. When he started the *Southern and Western Monthly Magazine and Review* (usually known as *Simms's Magazine*) in January, 1845, Simms in the Prospectus emphasized the need for a regional organ: "It is frankly avowed that the characteristics of the work are to be sectional."

[18]*Letters*, II, 90. In I, 319, he protested to G. F. Holmes that "Individually, I am no Anti-Anglican. I am so only in a purely national point of view."

[19]*Letters*, II, 75.

[20]*Views and Reviews*, I, 7. In "American Criticism and Critics," *Southern Literary Journal*, II (July, 1836), 396, he praised the *Knickerbocker* for pursuing "an indulgent course towards the infant literature of this country. . . . Certainly there is charity, a Christian virtue, if not criticism, in a course like this." But Simms, as noted above, very soon changed this opinion of the *Knickerbocker*.

[22]*Letters*, I, 187, 246, 320-22, 321n, and 324.

[23]*Letters*, II, 115-17.

[24]Miller, *The Raven and the Whale*, 107. See references to *Letters* immediately above; also II, 13-19, 28-29. In asking that publishers send books for review in the *Southern and Western*, Simms wrote (p. 29): "Of course while I shall be genial and indulgent, I shall always endeavour to be just."

[25]Simms' discussion of humor is in the article on Cornelius Mathews in *Views and Reviews*, II, 170-78. The quotations are, in order, on 170, 172, 174, 177, 178.

[26]Simms also praised very highly J. G. Baldwin's *Flush Times* as "full of fun and spirit," yet giving a realistic account of frontier life (*SQR*, NS IX, 555). In a "Lorris" Letter, Charleston *Mercury*, December 16, 1854, he describes it and *Party Leaders* as "a lively series of sketches . . . in a free, dashing hand, enlivened with anecdote, full of life, racy, witty, never tedious, and always truthful. The ease, freshness, and vivacity of these sketches deserve all praise, and will find few rivals to approach them." Near the conclusion of the unpublished 41-page manuscript, "Wit and Humor of the Professions," in the Charles Carroll Simms Collection, he also praises Baldwin and A. B. Longstreet for their use of legal humor in which "the lawyer is frequently a conspicuous person of the Drama." He had milder praise for W. T. Thompson's *Major Jones's Courtship* (*Magnolia*, June 1843, 399), and for J. J. Hooper's *The Widow Rugby's Husband* (*SQR*, NS X, 525-26). He also wrote an appreciative review of Francis Bailey's *Life of William T. Porter*, "a very clever man" whose *Spirit of the Times* "we believe . . . did good." (Charleston *Mercury*, Oct. 6, 1860).

[27]*Views and Reviews*, I, 12-13.

[28]*Views and Reviews*, I, 5-6. Simms did not think that the "American author should confine himself exclusively to the boundaries of his own country. Every man of genius has a certain character of independence, any attempt to confine which, would be as detrimental to his genius as it would be derogatory to his independence. This independence imparts to his mind an impulse, whose operations are very much like those of instinct.

. . . We should regard the doctrine of resolutely restraining ourselves to the national materials as being rather slavish than national, unless the native tendencies of the writer's mind carried him forward in their peculiar contemplation. But, at the same time, it must be remembered that the national themes seem to be among the most enduring." (*Views and Reviews,* I, 36).

[29] *Views and Reviews,* I, 16-17.

[30] Simms wrote four articles on "Copyright Law," in the *Southern Literary Messenger,* X (Jan., March, June, and August, 1844), 7-17, 137-51, 340-49, and 449-69. Simms' article took the form of letters to his friend George Frederick Holmes. Edward DeLeon of Columbia, South Carolina, had an article on "Cheap Literature" in the January issue, 33-39; it was a plea for an international copyright law and an attack on current American publishing practices. J. B. Dabney in the April (193-99) and May (289-96) issues denied the need for and the value of a copyright law. DeLeon answered Dabney in July (415-22). Holmes had a series, "The Present State of Letters," in the July (410-15) and September (358-42) issues. Simms wrote to the publisher, Edward L. Carey (*Letters,* I, 401), that "I am advised by my friends in New York and elsewhere that the cause of copyright is prospering and the argument making its way. I have no doubt myself that nothing short of this measure will save either American authors or American publishers." And he wrote in the *Southern Patriot,* Sept. 9, 1845, that reputable publishers not only wanted the copyright law but were beginning to welcome American authors. However, he confessed to DeLeon (*Letters,* I, 423): "I do not see that any present good will come of our arguments and expostulations, but 'good seed, well sown, they say, will bring its fruitage in no distant day'."

[31] *SLM,* X, 7.

[32] *SLM,* X, 11-13. In the *Southern Patriot,* July 9, 1846, Simms indicated his belief that if American writers were given proper encouragement, "It may be that the next great literary sensation will take place this side of the Atlantic."

[33] *SLM,* X, 13-14.

[34] *SLM,* X, 15-17, 137-44. Simms did not agree with many critics that cheap literature meant immoral and salacious literature. True, it gave wide circulation to the *Mysteries of Paris,* "that work equally prurient and powerful" (p. 149), and to the writings of Paul de Kock, "which I never allow myself to read"; but it also made readily available Froissart's *Chronicles* and other standard works. A considerable part of Simms' articles are devoted to practical aspects of book-making and publishing. In four "Lorris" Letters (Charleston *Mercury,* Jan. 6, 8, 10, and 12, 1855) Simms notes various improvements: The books are reasonably well made; many are copyrighted books by native authors; many are useful works on household problems, cookery, and even some sermons; many are good novels by relatively unknown authors; many are standard biographies, memoirs, and histories. These cheaply-produced books are widely sold and tremendously influential, as *Uncle Tom's Cabin* has proved. Of the books surveyed, Simms especially enjoyed Barnum's *Autobiography* for its honesty of delineation of the "shrewd secret of his intellect and performance" (Jan. 8).

[35] *Letters,* III, 76-77.

[36] *SQR,* NS II (Sept., 1850), 199: He limited this, however, to fiction and non-fiction in which "there is a show of malignity." Discussing novels on slavery in the "Literary Docket," Charleston *Mercury,* August 20, 1859, he added quite justly: "We can listen patiently to Old England man and

New England man, in the discussion of an abstract principle. We do not desire to prevent any man's opinion."

[37]*Ibid.*, 32. He also wrote such books as his *History of South Carolina* (1840) and *Geography of South Carolina* with the hope of setting the record straight and arousing local pride; a typical review of Southern school books, SQR, NS I (Oct., 1852), 530, praises them because they "neither slur over the truth in our history, [nor] assault our institutions."

[38]*The Wigwam and the Cabin*, 4-5. In the *Magnolia*, IV (April, 1842), 251-52, he defended Southern magazines by claiming that "If we do not make *our* work national, it will be because we fail to make it *sectional*. . . . There never was a national literature yet that was not made up of the literature of distinct sections."

[39]*Letters*, II, 310. The letters to James Henry Hammond are invaluable for revealing Simms' increasing pre-occupation with politics. On Christmas Day, 1846 (*Letters*, II, 242-43), he wrote to Hammond that "In my instance, you are probably correct in assuming that the novelist hurts the politician. . . . I flatter myself that our folk are beginning to know me— quite as much as a politician as they do as a novelist." A typical preamble opened his discussion of New Publications in the Charleston *Mercury*, October 3, 1860: "We have, in our official capacity, been somewhat regardless latterly, of the claims of literature; yielding the most of our thoughts and leisure to the more prevalent demands of politics and commerce."

[40]*Letters*, I, 196-97; *Magnolia*, III, (Jan., 1841), 1-6.

[41]*Ibid.*, 199-200. A year later, also in the *Magnolia*, IV (Jan., 1842), 63, Simms was asking, "When shall we find such articles in our American Periodicals, as that of Macaulay's on the *Life of Warren Hastings* in the last Edinburgh Review?" It would not be soon, he implied, for American writers "have to contend with three obstacles, the want of good and sufficient libraries, the fact that most of our literary men are bound down to the duties of some profession, and because there is no adequate compensation."

[42]*Letters*, I, 370. See also *Letters*, V, 388.

[43]*Letters*, V, 408.

[44]*Letters*, II, 516. He believed firmly that the "great secret of mental activity, in most countries, is the denseness of their settlements." When Nathaniel Beverley Tucker reviewed Macaulay's *History of England* for the SQR, Simms praised the manuscript for its thorough scholarship: "To Mr. Educated Gentleman, you have said all that is necessary. . . . But our masses require something more, and a review in all countries now acts in a two-fold position. It acts as a tribunal of criticism and as a summary of history. It embodies usually a general view of the whole subject" (*Letters*, II, 525). In "A Conversation with Hayne and Bruns," Charleston *Mercury*, September 9, 1859 (after complimenting Hayne's poetry and Dr. J. D. Bruns' editing of a medical journal), Simms notes that a literary journal "appeals to no profession," and not even to enough amateurs to support it: "An agricultural state may produce the great genius, but can never support or mature it. It must go elsewhere—must go to the great city."

[45]*Letters*, II, 519-21. Simms devoted many magazine editorial notes and even more newspaper columns to discussing current American and foreign periodicals, frequently discussing at some length the articles that interested him. Thus, in an article, "The European Periodical Press," Charleston *Mercury*, January 18, 1855, he notes that periodicals best illustrate the European mind; anyone interested must resort to those of Great Britain, France, and Germany. In the July 12, 1859, *Mercury*, he discussed nineteen

periodicals. The article, entitled "American Criticism and Critics," in the *Southern Literary Journal*, II (July, 1836), 393-400, is really a discussion of the editorial and critical policies of American periodicals. In a footnote Simms argues the case for "little journals. . . . They have their uses, and furnish some few of the first fields for exercise to the young and immature writer, whose crude and early compositions could not find their way into more elaborate and nicely-critical periodicals. In the history of literature—particularly in the formation of a national literature—no periodicals can be more valuable than these, and we should be indulgent to them, and they should be encouraged. It is necessary that young beginners should have frequent exercise in such vehicles, though it is something of a standing notion that young beginners should not publish at all until they are old. This is idle enough. How are they to avail themselves of criticism—how learn that most essential of all lessons, and which, unless he learns it, and learns it rapidly, no author can ever become successful— the art of self-criticism?"

⁴⁶*Russell's Magazine*, III (April, 1858), 36-47.

⁴⁷"Literary Prospects of the South," *Russell's Magazine*, III (June, 1858), 193-206, esp. 193-94.

⁴⁵*Letters*, IV, 412-13.

⁴⁹Preface, *War Poetry of the South*, v.

⁵⁰E. A. Duyckinck, *National Portrait Gallery of Eminent Americans*, I, 514. Simms complained in 1858 (*Letters*, IV, 40) that "I have so neglected my French and Italian that it is pretty hard work for me to read a page understandingly without a dictionary." But about 1850 he wrote to James Warley Miles (*Letters*, V, 326) that Augustus Sachtleben "has got back and proposes that we shall resume our German readings—the old class. We are to meet at my wigwam on Thursday night at 8 P. M. and look to see you there. We now propose to take up the Egmont of Goethe." In 1859, he recommended that Hammond get, in the original or in Leigh Hunt's "admirable translation," Francesco Redi's poem, "Bacco in Toscana" (*Letters*, IV, 133) "You may remember my telling you of Redi, expressing a wish to translate his 'Bacco in Tuscany,' and to add to it a fellow poem on the grapes of the South." A month later he wrote (IV, 143): "Redi's poem runs in my head, and if I can find, or invent, high sounding names for our wines and grapes, I propose to incorporate the matter into verse, in the irregular measures, and playful fancies of the Italian poet." Always interested in travel books, he praised William Dean Howells' *Italian Journeys* (Charleston *Courier*, Feb. 1 and 8, 1868) as an agreeable way "to visit Italy by proxy," since the author is "very good at detailed description, and paints with a free hand."

⁵¹*Southern Literary Gazette*, I (Sept., 1828) 6.

⁵²*Southern Literary Messenger*, X (June, 1844), 341.

⁵³*Letters*, IV, 127-28. See note 410. Almost forty years later (Charleston *Courier*, May 23, 1866) he used Matthew Arnold's *Essays in Criticism* as a springboard for contrasting English civilization unfavorably with French and especially German civilizations, although he describes this as a "charming book, graceful, scholarly, interesting," and Arnold as "a good poet, lacking creative energy." He had "an imagination more delicate than vigorous, and a culture of perfect finish."

⁵⁴Editorial Bureau, *Southern and Western*, I (Feb., 1845) 150. In the Charleston *Mercury*, December 22, 1860, he defended Balzac as a moral writer, and declared that "France has produced few greater moralists."

⁵⁵Charleston *Mercury*, May 24, 1860.

⁵⁶Of Lamartine as biographer, Simms wrote (Charleston *Mercury*, Decem-

ber 29, 1854): "His profundity lies in the proper enunciation of his own tastes, and in bringing out to a clear light, what of taste and sentiment lies at the bottom of the character which he portrays"; of Lamartine as historian (Charleston *Mercury*, May 31, 1855): "in spite of his *clinquant*, his meretricious eloquence, and more meretricious philosophies, the possession of taste, art, grace, and frequent beauty, especially of fancy, cannot be denied him." Reviewing *A History of Turkey*, Simms concentrates on its literary rather than its historical qualities.

[57]Simms thought it false to call *Toilers of the Sea* a novel (Charleston *Courier*, May 19, 1866): "Like all his later books, it is a violent and bitter assault upon society, religion, nature." But it had such tremendous power that he deemed it "the best of Victor Hugo's productions," including *Les Miserables*.

[58]"Carlyle's Writings," Charleston *Mercury*, June 22, 1860. Simms admitted that Carlyle sometimes abused the language, but felt that his "eccentricities of style" often contributed to "the force of the argument and the beauty of the illustrative portions." Simms had high respect for him as a thinker: "the mind of Carlyle, his native thought, the simple and stern shrewdness of his reasonings, the honest directness of his aim, his great sagacity, the fact that he rarely wrote without a moral purpose, all combined to render him triumphant in popular esteem." Although he had constructed no philosophical system, he had observed current wrongs keenly and passionately: "He laments in poetic diction as grand and terrible as that of Jeremiah." His grand affirmative he "resolved into the single word 'sincerity'. . . . the curse of mankind is that men will not be honest. . . . Perhaps Mr. Carlyle has never done more good to mankind than in the steadiness with which he has concentrated his great powers upon the inculcation of the one grand absorbing moral law of sincerity'."

[59]J. Wesley Thomas, "The German Sources of William Gilmore Simms," in *Anglo-German and American-German Crosscurrents*, I: 127-53. I am also indebted to Dr. Thomas for calling my attention to an unpublished dissertation by William W. Betts, Jr.: "The Fortunes of Faust in American Literature," 190-203 (Pennsylvania State University, 1954). The quotation from Thomas is on 139.

[60]"German Literature," *Southern Literary Gazette*, NS I (June, 1829) 197-201.

[61]Review of Goethe's Essays on Art, *Southern and Western*, II (Dec., 1845), 423-24. Simms drew heavily on an article in the *American Quarterly Review;* he thought poorly of Bodmer and Gottsched as poets and translators, but praised highly Albert Haller, Frederick Klopstock, and Lessing.

[62]See Thomas and Betts, note 410 above.

[63]*Views and Reviews*, II, 151. Simms did not like Bulwer-Lytton's translation, *The Poems and Ballads of Schiller*, for Schiller's poems, "sung ever from the heart within him," are antithetical to the "artificial requisitions" of Lytton's genius. In the Charleston *Mercury*, July 9, 1856, he discussed a translation of Schiller's *Don Carlos*, making objections to the renderings. See also *Letters*, IV, 408.

[64]*See* note 59.

[65]*Carl Werner*, I, 8-9.

[66]Editorial Bureau, *Southern and Western*, 1 (June, 1845), 433, and II (Sept., 1845), 207-08. In reviewing the second volume, Simms called Richter "the most tricksy and original spirit of the literature of modern Germany."

[67]"Our Literary Docket," Charleston *Mercury*, Sept. 9, 1859. Hayne is invited to play on a lyre in Simms' possession that was once owned by Bürger. The figurative overtones are obvious.

[6]Editorial Bureau, *Southern and Western,* II (Oct., 1845), 287. In the *Southern Literary Gazette,* I (March, 1828), 357-63, Simms objected to a writer in the *Southern Review* assigning Fouqué "the preference over Sir Walter Scott" (360). He objected likewise to over-praise of J. H. D. Zschokke's *Veronica;* it is pleasing enough, but only "an imitation of Scott such as Mr. James produces monthly" (*Southern and Western,*) II (Sept., 1845), 215.

[69]See the article by Thomas (N. 59, above), and Alexander Jones, "A Source for William Gilmore Simms," *Journal of American Folklore,* LXX (Jan.-March, 1957), 66-69. Reviewing favorably James Clarence Mangan's *Poems* in the Charleston *Mercury,* February 16, 1861, Simms wrote that "we half incline to think that none of the translators of Schiller, Uhland, Tieck, Körner, Bürger, Goethe, Freiligrath, Fouqué, etc., have shown themselves so free, so bold, so true to their originals."

[70]*Views and Reviews,* I, 59-60, 67, 80. He was equally insistent that history and biography must be artistic. Most of our own histories are by dull men, "wholly deficient in imagination and art." W. H. Prescott's "secret consists chiefly in the exercise of the appropriate degree of art. His materials, in the main, are to be found in a thousand old volumes, available to other writers; but it was in his art that the lumbersome records became imbued with life. His narratives of the conquest of Peru and Mexico are so many exquisite pictures—action, scene, portrait, all harmoniously blended in beautiful and symmetrical connection. . . . The parts harmonize, the persons work together, and the necessary links preserved between them, the action is unbroken to the close. . . . Nothing is dwelt upon at length, but that which justifies delineation, either from the intrinsic value of the material, or from its susceptibilities for art." (*Southward Ho!,* 108; on 130 he objects to the "miserable abridgements that flood the country, and too frequently pervert the truth; but, at best, the tone, the spirit, of the history is sadly lacking.") Reviewing *The American Revolution* in the Charleston *Mercury,* August 10, 1858 he praised George Bancroft because he "does not interfere with the action. He simply lifts the curtain upon the successive scenes, and when they are over, he drops it. . . . This is the true dramatic method, and it imparts to history a dramatic interest. It is high art adapted to the purposes of history." The biographer must be equally accurate and dramatic; also, in "Kennedy's Life of Wirt," *SQR,* XVII (April, 1850), 235, Simms praised Kennedy's "modern practice of allowing his subject to say as much as possible for himself." He noted in the prefatory Advertisement to his *Life of Captain John Smith* that "As much of Smith's own language as could be employed has been made use of without scruple."

[71]*The Lily and the Totem,* IV-V. See also *Views and Reviews,* I, 68-69. In a series signed "Clytus" and entitled "Flights to Florida" (Charleston *Courier,* Feb. 27-May 9, 1867), Simms mentions a good many French and Spanish authorities on Florida, and states that before the war he had owned 100 volumes on the subject and had translated from the works of some of these writers. A few translations are extant, in the Charles Carroll Simms Collection.

[72]*Views and Reviews,* I, 68-69. See Stanley T. Williams, *The Spanish Background of American Literature,* I, 220-23, and especially his longer and more useful article, "Spanish Influences on the Fiction of William Gilmore Simms," *Hispanic Review,* XXI (July, 1953), 221-29.

[73]*Count Julian,* vi-vii. In *The Album,* which ran from July to December, 1825, Simms had devoted considerable space to translations from Spanish and French. His *Early Lays* (Charleston, 1827), 70, contains a translation,

"The Spanish Chief." On *The Album*, see John C. Guilds, "Simms' First Magazine," in *Studies in Bibliography*, Charlottesville, Virginia, 1956, v. 8:169-85.

[74]*Trent*, 15.

[75]*Poems*, 1, 306-20.

[76]*Vasconselos*, IV. On pages 1-2, he emphasized that his fiction was also true history: It is the province of romance, even more decidedly than history, to recall the deeds and adventures of the past. It is to fiction that we must chiefly look for those living and breathing creations which history quite too infrequently deigns to summon to her service . . . her offices are not the less legitimate . . . she supplies those details which the latter, unwisely as we think, but too commonly holds beneath her regard. . . . We shall employ, without violating, the *material* resources of the Historian, while seeking to endow them with a vitality which fiction only can confer."

[77]In a "Lorris" Letter, Charleston *Mercury*, May 17, 1856, he discusses J. G. Lockhart's *Spanish Ballads*, asserting "that the historical and romantic ballads of Spain are regarded as models of their kind; and that no translation compares with' that of Lockhart." Commending T. C. Reynolds for an unfavorable review of George Ticknor's *History of Spanish Literature* (*SQR*, II, 85-123, 273-313), Simms complained that "I found Ticknor, as you say, singularly dry and costive—cold and tame. . . . He is not capable of rising into enthusiasm or of yielding himself to the atmosphere of poetry and romance." His complaint about Arthur Helps' 4-volume *Spanish Conquest in America* (Charleston *Courier*, July 22, 1868) is that it is commendable, but "too much abridged."

[78]*Views and Reviews*, I, 96-97. Timrod made this point years later, in the July, 1859, *Russell's;* commenting on the article in the Charleston *Mercury*, July 12, 1859, Simms agreed with Timrod that it "is the fault of the people themselves . . . that we have no favor shown to literature."

Chapter VI   NOTES: A SUMMING UP

[1]Simms was by no means alone in making this distinction, and in this country Hawthorne's comments have been even more influential. But Simms' observations were independently made, and still have value.

[2]*Letters*, I, 156-57. Here, Simms was perturbed because Lawson proposed to write an article "finding fault with Bryant." Lawson's "rashness of judgment . . . tempts you to be too soon satisfied with the light you have upon a subject, and leads you to a decision before you have sufficiently examined it under all lights." In the Epilogue to *Metamora*, line 36, Lawson had written that "The critic's merit is to find a fault" (*Letters*, V, 436).

[3]*Egeria*, 19; second sentence quoted in Hubbell, *The South in American Literature*, 594. Simms' prescriptions may have been wise, but I find his advice to other writers the least attractive part of his reviews.

[4]*Letters*, II, 230. Simms later tried to interest various publishers in another collection of his critical articles, but without success.

Index

145

DATE DUE			
MAR 3 0 2001			
MAR 2 0 2001			
APR 1 0 2001			
			Printed in USA

HIGHSMITH #45230